Oxford International Lower Secondary

CW00920681

Computing
Student Book

Alison Page

Howard Lincoln

Karl Held

OXFORD

Contents

Introduction

Delivering computing to young learners

Oxford International Primary and Lower Secondary Computing is a complete syllabus for computing education for ages 5–14 (Years 1–9). By following the program of learning set out in this series, teachers can feel reassured that their students have access to the computing skills and understanding that they need for their future education.

Find out more at:
www.oxfordsecondary.com/computing.

Structure of the book

This book is divided into six chapters, for Year 7 (ages 11–12).

1 **The nature of technology:** Introduction to binary numbers, conversion and addition

2 **Digital literacy:** Understanding how to be responsible and avoid risks and dangers on the internet

3 **Computational thinking:** Using different programming languages and understanding how commands work

4 **Programming:** Using if structures in Python and finding and fixing errors

5 **Multimedia:** Planning, recording and editing a podcast

6 **Numbers and data:** Storing data in a data table and checking for errors

What you will find in each unit

- Introduction: An unplugged activity and a class discussion help students to start thinking about the topic.
- Lessons: Six lessons guide students through activity-based learning.
- Check what you know: A test and activities allow you to measure students' progress.

What you will find in the lessons

Although each lesson is unique, they have common features: learning outcomes for each lesson are set out at the start; learning content delivers skills and develops understanding.

Activity Every lesson involves one or more learning activities for the students.

Extra challenge Activities to extend students who are able to do more.

Test A short test of four questions, of progressive difficulty, to check students' understanding of the lesson.

Additional features

You will also find these features throughout the book:

 Word cloud The word cloud builds vocabulary by identifying key terms from the unit.

Be creative Suggestions for creative and artistic work.

Explore more Extra tasks that can be taken outside the classroom and into the home.

Digital citizen of the future Advice on using computers responsibly in life.

Glossary Key terms are identified in the text and defined in the glossary at the end.

Assessing student achievement

The final pages in each unit give an opportunity to assess student achievement.

- Developing: This acknowledges the achievement of students who find the content challenging but have made progress.
- Secure: Students have reached the level set out in the programme for their age group. Most should reach this level.
- Extended: This recognises the achievement of students who have developed above-average skills and understanding.

Questions and activities are colour-coded according to achievement level. Self-evaluation advice helps students to check their own progress.

Software to use

We recommend Python for writing programs at this age. For other lessons, teachers can use any suitable software, for example: Microsoft Office; Google Drive software; LibreOffice; any web browser.

Source files

 You will see this symbol on some of the pages.

This means that there are extra files you can access to help with the learning activities. For example, half-completed Python programs or spreadsheet files.

To access the files, go to **www.oxfordowl.co.uk** and navigate to the 'Oxford International Primary Programme' page then 'Oxford International Primary Computing'.

Teacher's Guides

For more on these topics, look at the Teacher's Guide that accompanies this book.

1 The nature of technology: Storing digital data

You will learn

▶ how text, images and audio can be stored as digital data by a computer

▶ how to convert between binary and decimal numbers

▶ how to add binary numbers.

A computer stores data in digital files. A digital file only contains the characters zero and one. In this unit you will learn how text, photographs and images can be turned into digital data so that they can be stored on a computer. You will convert everyday decimal numbers into digital data. You will use codes that will help you understand how computers store text as numbers. You will create simple images and convert them into digital data in the same way as a computer. You will discover how digital sound and video are created.

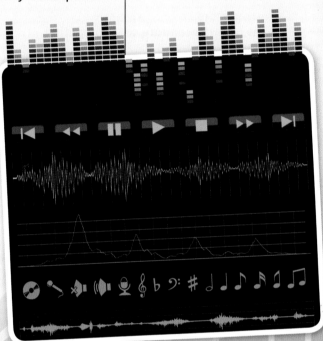

Talk about...

More of our personal data is being stored on the internet than ever before. We choose to store some of that information ourselves on social media sites. Governments, banks and online retailers save information about us online. Do you worry about your data being stored on the internet? Is your data safe?

Curriculum reference: Describe how different types of data can be represented in binary digital form; Convert between decimal and binary integers; Perform simple binary additions

🔌 Unplugged

Video and animation are created by showing a series of still images very quickly, one after the other. Create your own animation using a flick book. You will need 15 to 20 strips of paper stapled together. Draw a simple image on the first strip then change it slightly on each of the following strips.

An easy animation to draw is a bouncing ball. If you are feeling more creative, draw a dancing stick character. When you have finished, flick through the paper strips to animate your drawing.

Did you know?

Computers and other digital devices such as televisions display realistic-looking photographs and video images. Your computer uses a system called true colour to create realistic images. True colour allows the computer to store information about all the shades that make up an image.

True colour allows a computer to use more than 17 million colours in an image. That is more colours than most humans can see. Storing the information about a single true colour takes up the same amount of space as the computer uses to store the word 'red'.

binary   digital data   bit

byte   code   ASCII   media

pixel   true colour   sampling

Unicode

In this lesson

You will learn:

▶ what digital data is

▶ that computers store digital data as binary numbers

▶ how digital data is used to store numbers, media and instructions.

Spiral back

In Student Book 4 you learned about the different types of computer we can use to help us work and in our leisure time. All computers are digital devices – they store and process digital data. In this unit you will learn what digital data is and how computers use it to store text, images and sound.

Storing data

Humans store data – lots of data. We need to store data so that we can use it again when we need it.

People have stored data since ancient times. Early people stored data about important events by painting images on cave walls and by carving images and hieroglyphics into stone. Later people recorded their history and scientific achievements by writing on scrolls and parchment.

Throughout history, people developed different ways to store data. They developed printing so that they could store text and images in books. They developed vinyl records, tapes and then CDs to store and play music.

In the modern world, people use computers to store and process data. Most of the data that people use today is stored in a format that computers can use.

What is digital data?

When you communicate in English, you use letters and numbers. You use 26 letters and 10 digits, zero to nine. You also use punctuation characters such as the comma and full stop. You combine these characters to make words and sentences.

A computer stores data using only digits. Data that is stored using digits is called **digital data**. The computer uses only two digits: the numbers zero (0) and one (1).

Every file stored on a computer is made up of zeros and ones. A computer can use digital data files to store text, images, video or audio.

What does a computer use digital data for?

The 1s and 0s inside the computer can be used to store:

▶ yes and no (or true and false)

▶ numbers

▶ instructions that tell the computer what to do

▶ other digital content such as text, images and sounds.

Binary numbers

When you do use maths to solve day-to-day problems, you use the decimal number system. The decimal system has 10 different digits: the digits 0 to 9. The 'dec' in the word 'decimal' means 10. Some people think that we started to use the decimal system because we use our 10 fingers to count with.

The number system that a computer uses has two different digits: 0 and 1. This is called the **binary** number system. The 'bi' in the word 'binary' means two.

A computer uses binary to store numbers.

Binary numbers are used in calculations in the same way as decimal values. The table shows some example values written as both decimal and binary numbers. They look different but they mean the same thing.

Decimal and binary numbers	
Decimal	**Binary**
1	1
8	1000
18	10010
100	1100100

 **Activity**

Look at the table of binary and decimal numbers. Describe any differences and similarities between decimal numbers and binary numbers that you notice.

Storing text using binary numbers

A computer uses binary to store media. Binary can store text, images, sound and even video. When a computer uses binary to store media it uses codes.

To a computer the word 'Hello' looks like this: 01001000 01100101 01101100 01101100 01101111.

Each set of eight digits is a code for a letter. The code for 'H' is 01001000. The code for 'l' is 01101100. The code for 'l' is used twice in the binary word because there are two 'l's in 'Hello'.

01001000	01100101	01101100	01101100	01101111
H	**e**	**l**	**l**	**o**

In an image, codes are used to represent colours. In a music file, codes can be used to represent different instruments. Complex photographs and music files are all stored as zeros and ones.

 **Activity**

Using the binary number codes in the word 'Hello', translate the word below into English.

01001000 01101111 01101100 01100101

Storing instructions using binary numbers

The instructions in computer programs are stored in binary. In Unit 3 you will write computer programs. The instructions are written using human alphabets and symbols. The instructions in a program must be converted into binary so that the computer can store and use them. Each binary instruction tells the computer to do a simple task.

 **Activity**

Your task is to program a robot to find its way through a maze. There are just four simple instructions that you can give to the robot. These instructions tell the robot which direction to move:

▶ one step left

▶ one step right

▶ one step up

▶ one step down.

The binary codes for these instructions are shown in the table on the right.

Action	Code
One step left	00
One step right	01
One step up	10
One step down	11

Use the binary codes to write the program for the robot. Your program should follow the arrows shown in the diagram below to follow the green path through the maze from the blue square to the red square. The first five instructions are:

01, 11, 11, 00, 11

These instructions mean: 'Move one step right. Move one step down. Move one step down. Move one step left. Move one step down.'

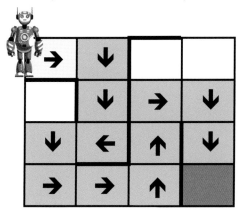

Complete the list of instructions to guide the robot to the red square.

Why do computers use digital data?

Computers are powered by microprocessors. The microprocessor is the 'brain' of a computer. A microprocessor is made up of millions of tiny electronic switches. The switches in a microprocessor are like any other switch. A switch can either be on or off.

A microprocessor is called a **digital** device because it can only understand the two switch positions – on and off. The on and off positions can be shown as 1 and 0 in binary. You have already learned that digital data is made up of 1s and 0s. That is why a digital microprocessor can read digital data.

 Extra challenge

Think about what you have learned in your computing course over the last year. List examples of activities and assignments where you have stored data as values, media and instructions to the computer.

✓ Test

1 Write down the two digits used in the binary number system.
2 Write down the eight extra digits used in the decimal system that are not used in binary.
3 In your own words, explain what digital data is.
4 Describe three things a computer stores as binary code.

In this lesson

You will learn:

▶ about bits and bytes

▶ how to convert binary numbers into decimal numbers

▶ the meaning of base 2 and base 10.

Understanding binary

Base 10 and base 2 numbers

In the last lesson you learned that a computer must store everything it processes as digital data. You learned that you can use the binary number system to understand what digital data looks like. You also compared some binary numbers to decimal numbers.

The decimal number system uses 10 digits (0 to 9). The value of each column in a decimal number is 10 times greater than the previous column. Another name for the decimal system is **base 10**.

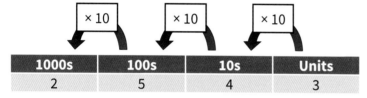

1000s	100s	10s	Units
2	5	4	3

The binary number system uses two digits (0 and 1). The value of each column in a binary number is 2 times greater than the previous column. Another name for the binary system is **base 2**.

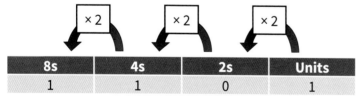

8s	4s	2s	Units
1	1	0	1

⚙ Activity

Other number systems are sometimes used in computing. One system is octal. Octal is the base 8 number system. Use the information you have learned about base 2 and base 10 to answer these questions:

▶ How many digits does the base 8 system use?

▶ What are those digits?

▶ What are the values of the first four columns in the base 8 number system? Draw a table to show your answer.

How to read binary numbers

You can use your knowledge of base 2 to read binary numbers. The easiest way to understand a binary number is to convert the binary number into a decimal number. You use the decimal system every day, so it is much easier to understand.

The binary number shown in the table above is 1101. Here is an easy way to convert the number into decimal.

1   Draw a table like the ones in the example on the previous page. It must have enough columns to hold the binary number you want to convert.

2   In the first row of the table, write the value of each column. Start with units in the right-hand column then multiply by 2 each time you move from right to left.

8s	4s	2s	Units

3   Write the number you want to convert in the second row of your table

8s	4s	2s	Units
1	1	0	1

4   Multiply each digit in the number you want to convert by the column value.

$1 \times 8 = \textbf{8}$ $1 \times 4 = \textbf{4}$ $0 \times 2 = \textbf{0}$ $1 \times 1 = \textbf{1}$

5   Add the results together. The total is the value of the binary number as a decimal number.

$8 + 4 + 0 + 1 = \textbf{13}$

1101 in binary is 13 in decimal.

 **Activity**

Convert these binary numbers into decimal numbers.

a   0111

b   1001

c   11001

d   111001

You will need to add more columns to the left-hand side of your table for the numbers in parts c and d. Remember that the value of each column must be 2 times the value of the column to the right.

Bits and bytes

Each digit in a binary number is called a **bit**. There are four bits in the binary number 1101. The word bit is short for '**b**inary dig**it**' – the first letter of 'binary' combined with the last two letters of 'digit'.

A bit isn't very useful on its own. It can only store one of two values: 0 or 1. To make binary more useful, computers group bits together. Eight bits grouped together is called a **byte**. Here are some examples of data stored in a byte: 11111111, 00000000, 00110101.

When you write a byte you must show all eight digits in the number, even if you have to start the number with zeros. The value zero as a byte is 00000000.

The language of numbers

'Ten' and 'eleven' are examples of names of numbers in the decimal system. Every number in the decimal system has a name. Numbers are not given names in binary. The binary number 11 is called 'one-one'. The decimal number eleven and the binary number 11 are different numbers.

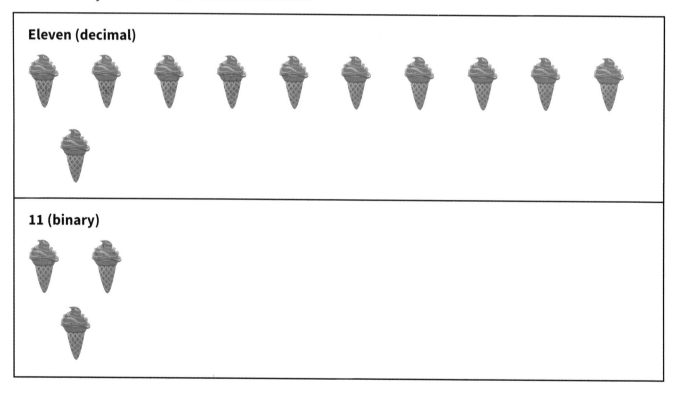

Eleven (decimal)

11 (binary)

⚙ **Activity**

Copy the table below and complete the column headings.

Then use the table to convert the byte 01100110 into decimal.

| | ×2 | | ×2 | | ×2 | | ×2 | | | | |

?	?	?	?	8s	4s	2s	Units
0	1	1	0	0	1	1	0

A binary to decimal shortcut

Base 2 is very easy to convert into decimal because it only uses two digits: 0 and 1. When you feel confident using the method of converting binary into decimal you have learned in this lesson, you can try this shortcut:

Use the byte table you created in the last activity. Start at the right of the binary number. Look at each digit in turn. Add together the place value of every column that contains a 1. With practice, you will soon learn the column heading values and be able to convert binary numbers in your head. Try this shortcut method when you complete the next activity.

 Activity

The table below contains the values 0 to 9 written as binary numbers. The numbers are in random order. Rewrite the list of numbers so that they are in order from zero to nine.

0011	0010	1000	0000	0110	0111	0101	0001	0100	1001

Extra challenge

Work with a partner or in two small teams.

Write each of the binary numbers from the table in the last activity on a separate card. Mix the cards up and lay them out facing your partner. Now set your partner some challenges.

▶ Point to a card and ask your partner to tell you the decimal value of the card.

▶ Pick three cards at random and ask your partner to place them in numerical order.

▶ Ask your partner to pick two cards that add up to the decimal value 6 (or choose another value).

✓ Test

1 Convert the binary number 1001 into decimal.

2 a What is a byte?

  b Convert the byte 11001011 into decimal.

3 Look at this binary number: 00100010. Explain why the 1 in column 6 has a different value to the 1 in column 2.

4 Explain what base 2 means.

Explore more

Teach a friend or family member how to read binary numbers. Challenge them to a contest.

In this lesson

You will learn:

▶ how to do simple addition in binary

▶ what overflow means when adding in binary.

When digital data is stored as a value it can be used in calculations. For example, you have used spreadsheets in this course. When you enter a formula such as =A3+B3 in a spreadsheet cell your computer will carry out binary addition. You have also learned programming in this course. When your computer moves a sprite on screen it uses binary addition to calculate a new position.

In this lesson you will learn how to do simple addition using binary.

Simple addition in decimal

To do addition in binary you use the same method as addition in decimal. It will help to look at an example of how addition works in decimal before moving on to binary addition.

If you lay out the addition in a table like the one on the right, it is easier to follow what happens when you add the numbers. You use the first two rows in the table for the numbers you will add together. You use the row at the bottom to record the sum. You use the shaded row to hold any values that you need to carry.

Number 1			
Number 2			
Carry			
Sum			

Example: decimal addition

In this example you will add together the numbers 262 and 174.

When you do an addition, you add together the numbers in each column from right to left and record the sum.

Step 1: Add the Units column: Add 2 and 4 together. Think of the sum as being '06'. This will help when you do binary addition later.

Write '06' in the table. Enter the 0 in the carry row of the 10s column. Enter the 6 in the sum row of the Units column.

	100s	10s	Units
Number 1	2	6	2
Number 2	1	7	4
Carry		0	
Sum			6

Step 2: Add the 10s column: The digits in this column add up to 13. Enter the 1 in the carry row of the 100s column. Enter the 3 in the sum row of the 10s column.

	100s	10s	Units
Number 1	2	6	2
Number 2	1	7	4
Carry	1	0	
Sum		3	6

Step 3: Add the 100s column: The digits in this column add up to 04. There is nothing to carry. Enter the 4 in the sum row of the 100s column. This completes the addition.

262 + 174 = 436.

	100s	10s	Units
Number 1	2	6	2
Number 2	1	7	4
Carry	1	0	
Sum	4	3	6

 **Activity**

Draw a copy of the table used in the previous example. Use it to add 729 and 252.

Adding in binary

You use the same method to add two binary numbers together. Adding in binary seems more difficult because you are not so familiar with binary numbers. There are four rules that will help you to do binary addition.

Rule 1: $0 + 0 = 00$			**Rule 2:** $0 + 1 = 01$		
Number 1		0	Number 1		0
Number 2		0	Number 2		1
Carry	0	0	Carry	0	0
Sum		**0**	**Sum**		**1**
Rule 3: $1 + 1 = 10$			**Rule 4:** $1 + 1 + 1 = 11$		
Number 1		1	Number 1		1
Number 2		1	Number 2		1
Carry	1	0	Carry	1	1
Sum		**0**	**Sum**		**1**

You can use these rules to add any two binary numbers. Write the two numbers one above the other so the bits line up. Start with the bits in the Units column (on the right). Look down the column. What bits do you see? It will be one of these possibilities:

▶ $0 + 0$

▶ $1 + 0$

▶ $1 + 1$

The rules of binary addition will tell you the answer. Write in the answer and any carry bit.

Now go to the next column (the 2s column). Look down the column, including any carry bit. What bits do you see? The same possibilities as before. Because of the carry bit there is another possibility:

▶ $1 + 1 + 1$

Write in the answer plus any carry bit. Do the same for every column until you have added every column.

You will see an example on the next page.

Example: binary addition

In this example you will add the binary numbers 0011 and 1011. You will use the four rules to help you with your binary addition.

Step 1: **Add the Units column:** Number 1 and Number 2 both have a 1 in the Units column. Rule 3 says 1 + 1 = **10**. Enter the 1 in the carry row of the 2s column. Enter the 0 in the sum row of the Units column.

Step 2: **Add the 2s column:** Number 1 and Number 2 both have a 1 in the 2s column. There is also a 1 in the carry row. Rule 4 says 1 + 1 + 1 = **11**. Enter the first 1 in the carry row of the 4s column. Enter the second 1 in the sum row of the 2s column.

Step 3: **Add the 4s column:** Number 1 and Number 2 both have a 0 in the 4s column. There is a 1 in the carry row. Rule 2 says 0 + 1 = **01**. Enter 0 in the carry row of the 8s column. Enter 1 in the sum row of the 4s column.

Step 4: **Add the 8s column:** Rule 2 says 0 + 1 = **01**. You don't need to enter the 0 because there are no more columns. Enter 1 in the sum row of the 8s column.

Step 1 Rule 3: 1 + 1 = 10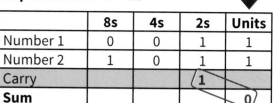

	8s	4s	2s	Units
Number 1	0	0	1	1
Number 2	1	0	1	1
Carry			1	
Sum				0

Step 2 Rule 4: 1 + 1 + 1 = 11

	8s	4s	2s	Units
Number 1	0	0	1	1
Number 2	1	0	1	1
Carry		1	1	
Sum			1	0

Step 3 Rule 2: 0 + 1 = 01

	8s	4s	2s	Units
Number 1	0	0	1	1
Number 2	1	0	1	1
Carry	0	1	1	
Sum		1	1	0

Step 4 Rule 2: 0 + 1 = 01

	8s	4s	2s	Units
Number 1	0	0	1	1
Number 2	1	0	1	1
Carry	0	1	1	
Sum	1	1	1	0

 Activity

A student wanted to add 1010 + 0010. They put the numbers into the addition table.

	8s	4s	2s	Units
Number 1	1	0	1	0
Number 2	0	0	1	0
Carry				
Sum				

Copy the table. Use the rules of binary addition to complete the table and find the sum.

Now use the same method to add 0011 + 0111.

Adding bytes

In the example of binary addition in this lesson, you added together two four-bit binary numbers. The method works for binary numbers with any number of bits. You learned in Lesson 1.2 that computers use bytes to store and process data. A byte is 8 bits long. To add bytes together, extend the table used in the example so that it holds 8 bits.

 **Activity**

A student wanted to add two 8-bit binary numbers:

00110111 + 01001010

They extended the addition table to eight columns and put the two numbers into the table.

	128s	64s	32s	16s	8s	4s	2s	Units
Number 1	0	0	1	1	0	1	1	1
Number 2	0	1	0	0	1	0	1	0
Carry								
Sum								

Copy the table. Use the rules of binary addition to complete the table and find the sum.

Now use the same method to add 01011001 + 00001111.

 Extra challenge

In this section you carried out a lot of binary calculations. You can check the results for yourself:

▶ Look at the two binary numbers you added together. Convert them both into decimal numbers.

▶ Look at the binary number that is the result of the addition. Convert that into a decimal number.

Now you have three decimal numbers. Add the first two numbers together. The result should equal your third number. If it all matches then your binary addition is correct.

Check all your binary addition sums using this method.

✓ **Test**

1   What is 1 + 1 in binary?

2   What are the four rules of binary addition?

3   Complete this binary addition: 00101101 + 00100101

4   Convert all the numbers in the sum in question 3 to decimal.

In this lesson

You will learn:

▶ how to convert between decimal and binary

▶ what an overflow error is.

When a decimal value is stored in the computer it must be converted to binary. In this lesson you will learn to convert decimal numbers into binary.

Place values

The 1s of a binary number have different values depending on their place in the number. You have learned to show those values as column headings.

Here is an example. It shows the binary number 00100100. The digits have been placed a table with all the column headings.

128s	64s	32s	16s	8s	4s	2s	Units
0	0	1	0	0	1	0	0

You can find the value of each 1 by looking at the column headings. The first 1 is in the 32s column. It has the value 32. The second 1 is in the 4s column. It has the value 4. You can find the total value of the number by adding up the place values. In this case, 32 + 4 = 36.

So the binary number 00100100 has the decimal value 36.

Convert decimal to binary

You can use the same number table to convert any decimal number to binary.

▶ Start at the left of the table.

▶ Subtract the place values from the decimal number (without going below 0).

▶ Whenever you subtract a value put a 1 into the table.

▶ Put 0 in all the other columns.

Worked example 1

Here is a worked example. You will convert the decimal number 20 into binary.

First draw the grid.

128s	64s	32s	16s	8s	4s	2s	Units

Start at the left. The first value is 128. That is too big to subtract from 20. So put a 0. Count along until you find a value that you can subtract. That is 16.

Put 1 into the 16s column.

128s	64s	32s	16s	8s	4s	2s	Units
0	0	0	1				

Subtract 16 from 20, and there is 4 left. Put 1 into the 4s column.

128s	64s	32s	16s	8s	4s	2s	Units
0	0	0	1	0	1		

You have now got 0 left so fill up the rest of the table with 0s.

128s	64s	32s	16s	8s	4s	2s	Units
0	0	0	1	0	1	0	0

So 20 in decimal is 00010100 in binary.

Worked example 2

Convert the decimal number 165 into binary.

Counting from the left we can subtract values like this:

165 – 128 = 37

37 – 32 = 5

5 – 4 = 1

1 – 1 = 0

The numbers subtracted are 128, 32, 4 and 1. Put 1s into these columns.

128s	64s	32s	16s	8s	4s	2s	Units
1		1			1		1

Put 0s in the other columns.

128s	64s	32s	16s	8s	4s	2s	Units
1	0	1	0	0	1	0	1

So 165 in decimal is 10100101 in binary.

Activity

Convert the following decimal numbers to binary. Show your working.

a 32

b 80

c 69

d 133

The largest number

In this unit you have learned to make numbers with up to 8 bits. That is 1 byte.

▶ The smallest number you can make with 8 bits is 00000000. That has the decimal value 0.

▶ The biggest number you can make with 8 bits is 11111111.

What is the decimal value of this number? You can find out by putting it into the binary grid.

128s	64s	32s	16s	8s	4s	2s	Units
1	1	1	1	1	1	1	1

128 + 64 + 32 + 16 + 8 + 4 + 2 + 1 = 255

So the biggest decimal number you can make with 8 bits has the value 255.

What about other numbers?

In real life the computer needs to store numbers outside of this range.
For example:

▶ numbers bigger than 255

▶ negative numbers (smaller than 0)

▶ fractions and decimal values, such as 4.5.

The computer needs to use more than 8 bits (one byte) to store these numbers. In this unit you will only work with numbers from 0 to 255.

🔧 **Activity**

Which of these decimal numbers **cannot** be turned into a binary number using 8 bits?

a 99

b 222

c 260

d 499

Overflow error

If you try to store a number bigger than 255 using 8 bits then you will get an error. This is called an overflow error. In Lesson 1.3 you learned about binary addition. Sometimes the result of a binary addition will be a number that is bigger than 255. In this case you will get an overflow error.

Worked example

Add the binary numbers 10101000 + 01100001.

Put them into the addition grid. Carry out the sum using the rules of binary addition.

	128s	64s	32s	16s	8s	4s	2s	Units
Number 1	1	0	1	0	1	0	0	0
Number 2	0	1	1	0	0	0	0	1
Carry	1	1	0	0	0	0	0	0
Sum	**0**	**0**	**0**	**0**	**1**	**0**	**0**	**1**

The final column is the 128s column. There are two 1s in this column. The rules of binary addition tell us that 1 + 1 = 0 and carry 1. But there is nowhere to put the carry value. There are no more columns.

This causes an overflow error. The result is shown as 00001001. That is **not** the right answer to the sum.

 Extra challenge

Add the two binary numbers 11001011 + 00111111. Show the overflow error.

 Test

1. Convert the decimal number 67 to binary.

2. What is the largest decimal number that can be shown using 8 bits?

3. Complete the following binary addition, showing the overflow error.

   01011100 + 11001000

4. Convert the following decimal numbers into binary and show that adding them together causes an overflow error.

   150 + 120

In this lesson

You will learn:

▶ how numbers are stored as digital data

▶ how text is stored as digital data.

What is a value?

You use numbers every day. Some of those numbers are used in calculations. For example, you add or multiply the numbers together. This type of number is called a **value**.

Other numbers are not values. A phone number is not a value. You don't add phone numbers together or subtract one phone number from another.

When these two types of number are stored as digital data they are stored in different ways.

Activity

Discuss with your group which of these numbers are values and which are not values. Report your findings to the class.

a your house number

b the number of marks you get in a test

c your age

d the number of points your team scores in a basketball game.

Other types of content

Number values are stored inside the computer using the binary number system. But what about other types of content? For example:

▶ text

▶ pictures

▶ sounds.

All of these types of content must be turned into numbers. Then the computer can store these numbers using the binary number system.

In the rest of this unit you will learn how the computer stores text, images and sounds as number values.

Storing text using ASCII code

Text characters include letters of the alphabet, punctuation marks, and other characters that you can type on a standard keyboard, such as spaces and maths symbols.

The computer uses a number code to represent these text characters. There is a common code used by almost all computers. It is called ASCII (ask-ee). Here are number codes for the letters a to g in lower case. Different codes are used for upper-case letters.

Character	Number code
a	97
b	98
c	99
d	100
e	101
f	102
g	103

How the computer uses ASCII code

When you press a key on the keyboard it sends a signal to the processor. The signal varies according to which character you selected on the keyboard.

When the processor receives the signal it stores the character using ASCII code. It stores the binary number. So, for example, the letter 'a' is stored as the binary number 01100001. The letter 'b' is stored as binary number 01100010, and so on.

Each ASCII code takes up exactly 1 byte (8 bits).

 **Activity**

Make an ASCII table.

a Copy the ASCII table in your book.

b Extend the table to show the whole alphabet from a to z.

c Add an extra column to the table to show the binary number for each character.

Use the ASCII table.

▶ Write your first name in ASCII using decimal values.

▶ Write your first name in ASCII using binary values.

Storing other characters

You have used ASCII to represent lower-case letters from a to z. ASCII can also be used to store upper-case letters and other keyboard symbols such as punctuation marks.

The next table shows the ASCII codes for some common keyboard characters.

Keyboard character	ASCII code (decimal)	ASCII code (binary)
Space	32	
Comma	44	
Full stop	46	

Activity

a Copy and complete the ASCII table to show the binary codes for the three keyboard characters.

b Here is a message in decimal ASCII. What does it say?

101 118 101 114 121 032 099 111 109 112 117 116 101 114 032 117 115 101 115 032 116 104 105 115 032 099 111 100 101

c Here is a message in binary ASCII. What does it say?

01111001 01101111 01110101 00100000 01110111 01101001 01101110

Numbers in ASCII

The digits from 0 to 9 also have ASCII codes. The ASCII code for a digit is not the same as its number value.

Keyboard character	ASCII code (decimal)	ASCII code (binary)
0	48	
1	49	
2	50	
3	51	
4		
5		
6		
7		
8		
9		

The computer can store a number using ASCII or as a number value. Different types of software store numbers in different ways.

▶ If you type the number 39 into a word-processed document, the computer will store the ASCII codes for 3 and 9. You cannot do a calculation using a word processor.

▶ If you type the number 39 into a spreadsheet, the computer will store the number value 39. You can do calculations using a spreadsheet.

 **Activity**

Copy and complete the number table to show the ASCII codes for all the digits from 0 to 9.

A problem with ASCII

There are only 256 characters in ASCII. ASCII was originally created to convert from English into binary. However, people around the world need to use computers in their own language.

An improved code called **Unicode** was invented in 1991. Around 110,000 characters are available in Unicode, including the ASCII codes. Unicode has codes for characters in Arabic, Mandarin and Japanese, as well as many other languages.

▶ ASCII uses a single byte to store the code for each character. The maximum number of characters a single byte can hold is 256.

▶ Unicode uses more than one byte to store characters. Two bytes joined together can hold 65,000 characters. Three bytes joined can hold nearly 17 million characters.

 **Activity**

Work with a partner. Write a short message in ASCII with about 10 characters and no punctuation. Give your message to your partner to decode. Work together to check you have coded and decoded each message correctly.

 Extra challenge

Search the web to find a full ASCII character code table. Make sure that the table includes the binary codes. Look at the ASCII codes for lower-case and upper-case letters. Explain how they are different.

✓ **Test**

1 What does 24 look like when it is stored as:
   a a value in binary?
   b ASCII?
2 When you type a character on your keyboard, what data is sent to the computer?
3 Why is ASCII limited to 256 characters?
4 What advantages are there to using Unicode instead of ASCII?

In this lesson

You will learn:

▶ how images are converted into digital data

▶ how audio sounds are converted into digital data.

Everything you store on a computer must be stored as digital data. In the last lesson you learned how numbers and text are stored as digital data. Images, sound and video are also converted into binary so that a computer can store and use them.

Digital images

When you look at a photo on your computer screen it looks like the real world. In fact, it is an image made up of tiny squares called **pixels**. The word pixel is short for 'picture element'.

The pixels are organised in a grid of rows and columns. The picture is like a spreadsheet, but the cells contain colours not numbers. Each pixel stores a single colour.

Pixels are so small that you cannot see the individual squares. Your brain blends the individual colours together to create a realistic image. An image created in this way is called a bitmap. Most images you see on computer screens are bitmaps.

Each colour the computer uses has its own binary code. The computer uses a colour code chart to convert the colour of each pixel into a binary code.

Example 1: storing two colours

A simple image has been created on a square grid measuring 8 × 8 pixels. The image uses only two colours – black and white. All the information the computer needs to store the information about each pixel can be stored in a single bit.

If the pixel is white, the computer stores a 1 in the bit. If the pixel is black, the computer stores a 0. The computer can store all the information it needs about each line in this simple image using a single byte. The information looks like this:

11100111 11100111 11011011 00000000 11100111 10000001 00111100 01111110

 **Activity**

Draw a blank 8 × 8 pixel grid. Recreate the image stored in the digital data below. Work from the top left of the grid to the bottom right. 1 is a white square and 0 is black.

11111111 11100011 11011101 10101010 10111110 10100010 11011101 11100011

Images with more colours

Most images use more than two colours. In Example 1, a single digit was used to store information about the colour of a pixel. A single digit can store just two values. To store more colours, a computer uses more bits.

Example 2: storing more colours

In this example, the computer uses two bits to store the colour information about a single pixel. Using two bits means four colour codes can be used: 00, 01, 10 and 11. The codes used to store the colours in this example are: 00 black, 01 red, 10 blue and 11 white. The method is the same as in Example 1. Using more bits means you can use more colours in an image.

True colour

The examples in this lesson are simple images to explain how images can be stored as digital data. For most images, a computer uses more than two bits to store colour information.

For simple images like icons and emojis, the computer uses a byte (8 bits) to store colour information. A byte can store 256 different colours.

Photos need more than 256 colours to look realistic. A computer uses a method called **true colour** to store digital data about photos. True colour uses three bytes to store the information about a single pixel. True colour allows nearly 17 million colours to be used.

Realistic images

Using more colours makes an image look realistic. This is called **colour depth**. Adding more colours increases the colour depth.

Another way to make images more realistic is to use more pixels. This is called **resolution**. Using more pixels to display an image gives high-resolution images.

Low resolution

High resolution

Digital sound

If you press a piano key, a hammer strikes a string and the string vibrates. The vibration is a wave of sound that passes through the air to our ears. The sound wave is continuous and smooth.

A computer cannot save continuous data. The computer must break up continuous data into chunks that can be stored in bytes in its memory. This process is called **sampling**. A sample is a slice of the sound taken at a moment in time.

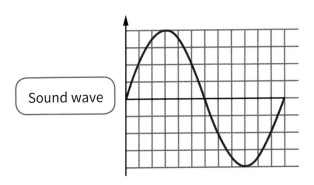

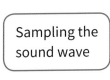

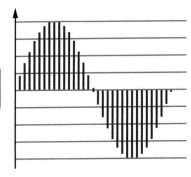

When sampling, the computer takes measurements of the continuous sound wave at regular intervals throughout the recording. The computer stores the measurements as digital data. The number of samples recorded per second is called the sampling rate. A piece of digital music is sampled around 44,000 times per second.

The sampling process never captures sound exactly. There are gaps between samples where sound is missed, but the gaps are so small that the digital sound appears continuous when we listen to it.

High-quality audio recordings have a high sampling rate. More samples are taken per second during the recording.

Digital video

Digital video is created in the same way as audio. Sampling is used to capture slices of an event that happens continuously. The slices are called **frames**. When frames are displayed quickly one after the other, we see an image moving as it would in real life.

Earlier in this unit you created a flick book animation. The activity simulated the way that video is captured and displayed as digital data.

When a video is stored as a digital file, the images and audio are saved separately using the methods described in this lesson.

 **Activity**

Create your own two-colour picture in an 8 × 8 grid.

Convert each line in your grid into a byte: white = 1, black = 0.

Exchange your binary code with a partner.

Use the binary code to redraw your partner's image.

 **Extra challenge**

Create an information sheet that explains how sampling is used to capture and store audio in a digital data file. Search the web to find an image and more information about sampling.

 Test

1   Explain in your own words how pixels are used to make a digital image.

2   Describe how sampling is used to capture audio on a computer.

3   How are colour depth and resolution used to create high-quality images?

4   High-quality image files are larger than low-quality files. Why is that?

Check what you know

You have learned

▶ how text, images and audio can be stored as digital data by a computer

▶ how to convert between binary and decimal numbers

▶ how to add binary numbers.

Try the test and activity. They will help you to see how much you understand.

Test

1 What are bits and bytes?

2 What is another name for the base 2 number system?

3 Show how to convert the decimal value 172 into binary.

4 Show how to add together the binary numbers 00011011 and 00101001. Do the same sum in decimal to check your answer.

5 Explain why the two 1s in this binary number do not have the same value: 00100010.

6 Explain what happens when you add these two bytes together: 01101010 + 10011000.

 **Activity**

Create a presentation to explain to other students how digital files are used to store text and images. Create the following slides for your presentation:

Slide 1: Explain that a computer stores everything as digital data.

Slide 2: Explain in your own words how a computer uses ASCII code to store letters in a digital file.

Character	Binary Code	Character	Binary Code
a	01100001	0	00110000
b	01100010	1	00110001
c	01100011	2	00110010
d	01100100	3	00110011
e	01100101	4	00110100
f	01100110	5	00110101
g	01100111	6	00110110
h	01101000	7	00110111
i	01101001	8	00111000
j	01101010	9	00111001

Slide 3: Explain how simple images can be stored as binary code in a digital file.

Slide 4: Explain how combining two or three bytes allows many characters or colours to be stored in a digital file. Use Unicode or true colour as an example. You can include information from your own web research on your slide.

Self-evaluation

- I have answered test questions 1 and 2.
- I have created Slide 1 for my presentation.
- I have answered test questions 1–4.
- I have created Slides 1–3 for my presentation.
- I have answered all the test questions.
- I have created a presentation with all four slides.

Re-read any parts of the unit you feel unsure about. Try the test and activity again – can you do more this time?

2 Digital literacy: Staying safe online

You will learn

▶ how to recognise the risks and dangers on the internet

▶ how to avoid risks and dangers on the internet

▶ how to use internet content responsibly.

In Student Book 5 you learned what it means to be a responsible internet user. Not everyone who uses the internet behaves responsibly. There are some people who make the internet a dangerous place. There are criminals who attempt to steal from you. Others try to install malicious software on your computer. There are bullies who use the internet to frighten and threaten people.

In this unit you will learn about the risks that the internet brings into our lives. You will learn the steps you need to take to guard against these risks.

 Unplugged

Answer these two questions individually. How much do you agree with each statement? Choose the answer that is true for you.

"I feel safe when I am online."	"I am confident that I know how to stay safe online."
1 I feel very safe.	1 I am very confident.
2 I feel quite safe.	2 I am quite confident.
3 I feel neither safe nor unsafe.	3 I am neither confident nor unconfident.
4 I sometimes worry I am at risk.	4 I don't know very much about staying safe.
5 I think the internet is a dangerous place.	5 I know nothing about staying safe online.

Collect the responses of everyone in the class. Create a graph to present your class's responses.

Learning outcomes: Use content from online sources responsibly; Explain risks associated with internet use; Discuss how data may be collected when working online

CYBERCRIME

IDENTITY THEFT

HACKING

MALWARE

VIRUS

CYBERBULLY

RANSOMWARE

Talk about...

Some of the threats you face when using the internet are shown above. You will learn more about these threats in this unit, but you may already have heard about some of them. Share what you already know about these threats with your group.

Which of the threats do you worry about most? What do you do to stay safe online?

Did you know?

By 2021 the cost of internet crime is expected to be $6 trillion a year. Businesses across the world will spend $1 trillion to protect themselves against criminals who use the internet.

cybercrime

hacking   malware   cyberbully

anti-virus software   internet shopping

e-commerce   secure site   cookie

intellectual property   copyright

plagiarism   firewall

In this lesson

You will learn:

▶ how data is collected online

▶ how cookies are used on websites.

Finding information online

There are many reasons to look for information. You might do a web search to find information for a geography project. You might look for reviews online to help you decide which model of smartphone is best for you.

In the modern world, the information you need is usually on the internet. When you use the internet you also give away information. In this lesson you will learn about the ways in which websites collect data about you.

Online registration

Websites such as social media and internet shopping sites usually ask you to register before you can use them. **Registration** means becoming a member of a website. You fill in an online form and provide information about yourself to the owner of the site.

In return for registering, you receive some benefits. For example, you might be able to:

▶ read pages that are hidden from non-registered users

▶ leave messages in chat rooms and on message boards

▶ add content

▶ get email updates when new content is added to the site

▶ download software.

First name	
Last name	
Username *	
Email	
Password *	
Confirm password *	
Phone number	
Date of birth	

Submit

Which information should you give?

The owner of a website should only collect the information they need, such as a username and password. They may also need contact details such as an email address. Some websites ask for optional information such as your telephone number or birthday. You don't have to give optional information to register. Always think about what information you need to provide when you complete forms online.

 **Activity**

Imagine you have designed a new website about your favourite computer game. Your website has a chat room so that friends can discuss the game and share tips on how to play. What information will you collect from your friends when they register? Design a registration form to use on your website.

Online shopping

Buying online is called internet shopping or **e-commerce**. Internet shopping sites collect data when people buy things. Some of the data that shopping sites collect is personal data, including:

▶ bank details – so we can pay for the items

▶ address and other contact details – so the company can deliver the items.

Website owners must keep personal details safe. A criminal can use a person's bank details to steal money from their bank account. A criminal can use personal details such as a person's address to impersonate (pretend to be) the person and then commit crimes in their name.

Internet shops use **secure sites** to protect data. A secure site **encrypts** information that is sent over the internet. Encrypted data is coded. If a criminal steals the data they will not be able to read or use the data.

Is this site secure?

When you are browsing the web, there are two clues that tell you a website is secure.

There is a small locked padlock symbol.

The URL of a secure site starts with https://. The 's' stands for secure. It tells you that data is encrypted when it is sent over the internet.

Never send information across the internet if the website is not secure. However, not all secure sites are safe to use. The safest way to send information is to use a secure site that you have used before and can trust.

Cookies

A **cookie** is a small file that is stored on your computer when you visit a website. A cookie saves information about the way you use web pages. The website uses this information to improve your experience of using the website.

Cookies & Privacy

This website uses cookies.

By continuing to browse this website, you agree to our use of cookies.

Learn More

Types of cookies

There are four types of cookie.

▶ **Essential cookies** are needed to make a website work as designed. On an internet shopping site, the shopping basket function needs cookies to make it work properly.

▶ **Performance cookies** collect information about how you use a website. The owner of a website uses this information to improve the performance of the website.

▶ **Functionality cookies** record what you do on a web page. This information is used to personalise the web page for you.

▶ **Advertising cookies** record what you look at online. The information is used to personalise the adverts displayed on a web page.

What are cookies used for?

Cookies are used for two main reasons:

▶ Cookies make it easier to use websites. For example, if you complete a form on a website, the information is saved in a cookie. This means that the website can automatically complete the form the next time you use it.

▶ Cookies are used to personalise a website. For example:

● A cookie can store your location. That information can be used to make sure you see weather reports and events that are local to you.

● Advertisers use cookies to make sure they show you adverts for events and products you are interested in. They can collect this information from your browsing history.

● The news stories that you see can be customised to match your interests.

Did you know?

The first internet shop was called NetMarket. It made its first sale in 1994. In 2019, 1.92 billion people were expected to buy something on the internet.

Cookies and the law

The information that cookies collect is often very valuable to advertisers. Some website owners sell the information to advertisers and other organisations such as political parties. Some cookies have been developed to collect valuable information that can then be sold. These are called tracking cookies.

Some people worry that tracking cookies can be used to influence our opinions and affect the way we vote in elections.

The governments in some countries have passed laws about the use of cookies. Website owners must make it clear what cookies their sites use and what they use the cookies for. These laws make it easier for people to decide which cookies to accept and which to reject.

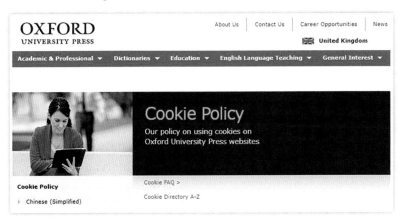

 **Activity**

Draw a table with two columns like the one shown here.

Good uses of cookies	Bad uses of cookies

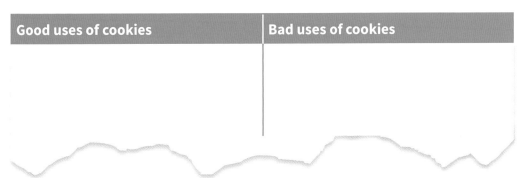

In the first column list all the ways that cookies make using the internet better. In the second column list all the bad things that cookies are used for.

 **Extra challenge**

Search the web to find out more information about cookies. Add any new information you discover to the table you created in the activity.

 Test

1 Name two reasons for data being collected online.
2 What are the two main reasons that websites use cookies?
3 Explain how cookies can be used to personalise a website. Give examples.
4 Why do people worry about the use of cookies on websites?

In this lesson

You will learn:

► about the risks you face online from cybercriminals.

Cybercrime

One risk you face on the internet is **cybercrime**. A **cybercriminal** is someone who uses the internet to commit their crimes. Some cybercriminals sell illegally over the internet. Some cybercriminals attempt to steal money and other possessions from people.

Cybercrime methods

Criminals use several methods to steal people's money and identities:

Identity theft – A criminal steals personal information such as a person's name and address. They also steal official information such as social security numbers or passport numbers. Criminals can use a stolen identity to pretend they are someone else. They can open a bank account or a credit card account in someone else's name. They then use these fake accounts to buy goods or to steal money from banks.

Phishing – A criminal creates a fake website that looks like the official website of a real bank or internet shopping website. The criminal then writes a fake email that looks like it comes from the bank or shopping website.

The email tells the person receiving the email that there is a problem with their account and they must log in to solve the problem. There is a link to the fake website. When the person logs in, the fake website records their username and password. The criminal can then use the person's login details to steal money.

Spiral back

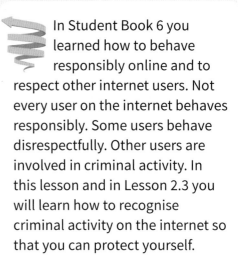

In Student Book 6 you learned how to behave responsibly online and to respect other internet users. Not every user on the internet behaves responsibly. Some users behave disrespectfully. Other users are involved in criminal activity. In this lesson and in Lesson 2.3 you will learn how to recognise criminal activity on the internet so that you can protect yourself.

Personal Data

Only a small percentage of people are fooled by phishing emails, but every victim can lose hundreds or thousands of dollars to the criminal.

Scamming – A criminal sends out an email that asks for money. Sometimes the email contains a threat that the victim owes money and will have to go to court if they do not pay the debt. Sometimes the email offers something for sale at a very low price or asks for a donation to a charity. Scammers also use social media sites.

If the criminal emails enough victims, someone will be fooled and will send money to the criminal.

Hacking – A criminal breaks into a computer system, usually to steal files or personal information. Hackers usually try to break into computer systems that hold a lot of personal information. Bank systems are an example of the type of system that hackers attack.

Did you know?

Banks and other organisations sometimes employ hackers to attempt to break into their systems. This can reveal weak spots where the system is insecure. The organisation can then fix the weak spots before a malicious hacker finds them.

Be creative

Create a poster that warns about the dangers of cybercrime. Use some or all of the key words from this lesson. Search the internet for a good image to illustrate your poster. Your poster can warn about all the dangers of cybercrime or it can focus on one type of cybercrime, such as identity theft.

Malware

Malware is software that a criminal installs on a computer. Some types of malware are designed to steal personal information. Other malware is designed to damage files or stop a computer from working properly. Some types of malware are:

▶ **Virus** – spreads and infects files that it meets. That makes a virus difficult to cure. Some viruses are relatively harmless – they make messages pop up on your screen, for example. Other viruses are more dangerous – they can destroy files and steal personal data.

▶ **Trojan** – malware that is hidden inside another program, for example in a game. When someone uses the program, the malware is released and starts to work. Trojans are popular with cybercriminals because they are easy to write and spread.

▶ **Ransomware** – encrypts all the data on a computer. That means that the data cannot be used. The victim of a ransomware attack receives a message demanding a payment to remove the encryption.

▶ **Spyware** – sits on a computer and records what the user is typing. Criminals can use spyware to discover login details.

▶ **Adware** – places unwanted adverts on a computer. The adverts are often displayed in another web page such as a social media or internet shopping site. Adware is not as damaging as other malware, but it can be annoying. If you have adware on your computer, it is a warning that your computer is vulnerable to other more dangerous malware.

Criminals often use email to spread malware. They often send fake emails with subjects that encourage you to open them. For example, the email subject might say you have won a prize in a competition or warn you that your computer has a serious problem you need to deal with.

The email encourages you to open or install a software application or open a document. The file contains malware, so when you open the file your computer is infected with the malware.

Did you know?

One of the most serious malware attacks was a ransomware attack called WannaCry. It affected over 200,000 computers in 150 countries. WannaCry closed important computer systems including some hospital systems, so the hospitals had to cancel operations. The cost of the attack was estimated at $4 to $8 million.

Activity

Read the Did you know? box. Search the internet to find out about other major malware attacks that have taken place. Choose one of the malware attacks that interests you. Write a brief description of the attack. Some things you can include in your description are:

▶ the name of the malware

▶ the type of malware

▶ the effect of the malware

▶ when the attack took place

▶ how many people were affected

▶ the cost of the attack

▶ the person or people responsible for the attack.

Extra challenge

Trojan malware is sometimes called 'Trojan horse' malware. Its name comes from an Ancient Greek story. Search the internet to find out what the original Trojan horse was. Why is the name Trojan horse used for this type of malware?

Test

1 Name three types of malware.

2 What is ransomware and why is it dangerous?

3 Explain why a stolen identity can be valuable to a criminal.

4 Describe how criminals use emails to spread malware.

In this lesson

You will learn:

▶ how to protect your computer against malware and hackers.

Anti-virus software

You can prevent malware from doing damage by installing **anti-virus software** (**AV software** for short) on your computer. AV software deals with all malware threats, not just viruses. AV software sits on your computer, looking out for malware.

How AV software works

Every piece of malware has a fingerprint. The fingerprint is a piece of programming code that is unique to the malware. This fingerprint is called a **signature**. AV software contains a database of malware signatures.

AV software continually checks the files on your computer, looking for malware signatures. If your AV software finds a malware signature in a file, it puts the file in **quarantine** – this means that the computer cannot open the file.

ScanPlus

Warning!

File Quarantined

mobilegames.hub.exe was detected as malware Susp.Win.Virus.Trlo-834305-2.

Quarantine was successful.

Modern AV software protects your computer very well. But there may be times when AV software fails to detect malware. If a new piece of malware is developed, your AV software will not recognise it because the signature of the malware will not be in the signature database.

AV software updates the signature database regularly. But there will always be times when your computer is vulnerable to new malware.

 **Activity**

There are many companies that make AV software. Norton and Kaspersky are two examples. Search the web for the names of other AV software packages. Find reviews of different brands of AV software. Make a note of the good and bad points in the reviews for each product.

Firewall

AV software detects and quarantines files that contain malware. Another type of software that protects your computer is a **firewall**.

A firewall surrounds and protects your computer like the walls of a castle. A firewall checks all data before it allows the data to pass through the gates in the wall. Only data that comes from a safe source can pass through the wall.

Your firewall and AV software work together to protect your computer from malware.

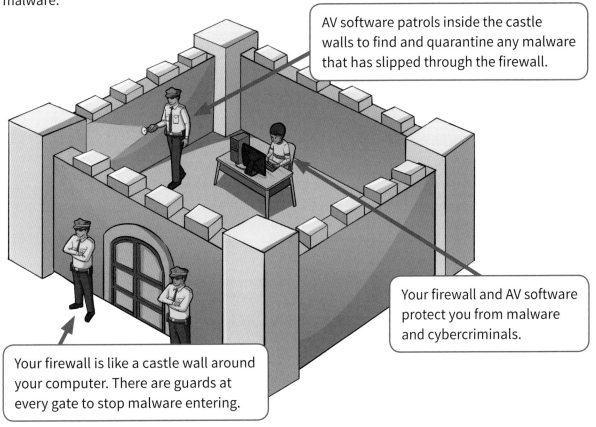

AV software patrols inside the castle walls to find and quarantine any malware that has slipped through the firewall.

Your firewall and AV software protect you from malware and cybercriminals.

Your firewall is like a castle wall around your computer. There are guards at every gate to stop malware entering.

Using your computer safely

You can improve your security by behaving responsibly and safely when you use your computer.

Use firewall and AV software

Never turn off the firewall or AV software on your computer. Never change any of the settings in the software. If you do, your computer is open to malware.

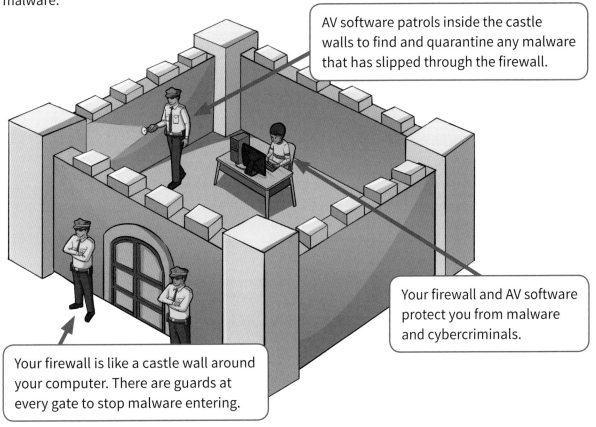

Use email safely

Malware can come from files attached to emails. If you open an email attachment, you may be inviting a criminal onto your computer.

Criminals and hackers use misleading email titles to tempt you to open a mail. For example:

"Congratulations! You have won first prize in our free draw."

"Warning! Your account is about to be closed. You MUST act now!"

Be wary of emails from people you do not know. Even emails that look genuine can be clever fakes. An honest email will never ask you to give away personal information or login details.

Use the web safely

When you are searching the web, only use sites that you trust. Files that you download can contain malware. Downloading apps and games is particularly risky. If you are downloading software, always use an official site.

When browsing the web, you will sometimes see messages that tell you there is a problem with your computer. The message will tell you that you need to download software to fix the problem. Do not download the software. Close the web page.

> **We have detected a problem with the virus protection on your computer.**
> **You should scan for viruses immediately.**
> **Download Virus Scanner**

Never click on links in messages that appear when you are online.

Update your software

Keep the software on your computer up to date. Software companies constantly check their software for errors. Sometimes they find security errors. Criminals and hackers use security errors to access computers.

If your software provider sends you an update message, update your software immediately. The updated version will make it more difficult for criminals to install malware. If you think an update message may be malicious, check with an adult before accepting it.

Spiral back

 In Student Book 5 you learned about using strong passwords. Always use strong passwords that are difficult for a hacker to guess.

Your software provider will send update messages to a window on your screen, never as an email message.

Keep your password safe

Use a strong password that contains upper and lower case letters, numbers and other characters (for example, $). A strong password should be at least eight characters long

Change your password regularly. That makes it more difficult for hackers to access your computer even if they do manage to steal your password. If you think your password has been stolen, change it immediately.

Keep your password secret. Never share it and don't write it down.

 **Activity**

Write a guide for students on how to work safely online and avoid the risk of malware.

 **Extra challenge**

In Student Book 5 you learned the passphrase method to create strong passwords. Search the web to find another method for creating a strong password. Write down instructions with an example. Add these to your guide on working safely online.

Did you know?

Hackers use special software to crack passwords. A weak password that is 7 characters long can be cracked in less than 1 second. A strong password that is 12 characters long could take 200 years to crack.

 Test

1 Name two types of software you can use to protect your computer from malware.

2 Why is it important to update the software on your computer regularly?

3 Explain how AV software and a firewall work together.

4 Explain why you need to be careful when you open a file attached to an email.

In this lesson

You will learn:

▶ that bullying can be a danger on the internet

▶ how cyberbullies work

▶ what to do if you experience cyberbullying.

What is cyberbullying?

A person who uses the internet to bully people is called a **cyberbully**. Cyberbullying is a serious problem. In some countries, over 50% of young people have experienced cyberbullying. Cyberbullying often takes place on social media sites, but bullies also use email and text messages.

Methods cyberbullies use

▶ **Harassment** – A bully sends threatening messages by text message or instant messaging. This is a serious form of bullying. The messages often make physical threats. They can be very frightening.

▶ **Impersonation** – A bully chooses a target (a person they want to bully) and then sends messages that pretend to be from the target. The messages are sent to people who know the target. The aim is to cause trouble between the target and their friends.

▶ **Exclusion** – A bully sends messages that publicly exclude the target from social groups and events. For example, the bully posts a message on a social media site saying that the target is not invited to an event.

▶ **Dissing** – A bully circulates rumours (untrue stories and opinions) about a target. The rumours are designed to humiliate and ridicule the target.

▶ **Photographs** – Some cyberbullies use their smartphone camera to take photos of a target. They then share the photos by text message or social media. They sometimes use the photos in harassment messages.

Be creative

Write a short story about cyberbullying. Choose one of the methods that cyberbullies use. Describe an incident when a bully used that method. How did the target feel about the bullying? What did they do about it? Why did the bully act that way?

The effects of cyberbullying

Cyberbullying is malicious and persistent. It can seem impossible to escape from. A bully can strike at any time, using text messages and social media posts. The internet brings the bullying into the target's home.

Bullying over the internet is often anonymous. Not knowing who is carrying out the bullying makes it more frightening. Cyberbullying can be devastating if you are the target. It can affect every aspect of life.

Confidence

No matter how much a target tries to ignore cyberbullying, the bullying will affect their self-confidence. Low self-confidence can lead to anxiety and depression. Being the constant target of rumour and ridicule makes a person feel powerless and vulnerable.

Loneliness

Being bullied is a lonely experience. A person who is bullied often feels that no-one can help them. They feel isolated, which may cause difficulties in their relationships with family and friends. The target of cyberbullying can withdraw from their family and social groups.

Performance at school

A target of bullying sometimes does less well at school. The cyberbullying distracts them from their schoolwork and they find it difficult to concentrate in class. In extreme cases the person may start to miss classes. They no longer enjoy learning or being with school friends.

Change of personality

Being bullied can change someone's behaviour and personality. A person who is usually pleasant and respectful may start to misbehave or become aggressive. The stress caused by bullying can also lead to problems with sleeping and eating routines. The person may even become ill.

What makes a cyberbully?

If you are the target of a cyberbully, it is easy to think that you are to blame in some way for the bully's actions. It is important to realise that you are not to blame. There are many reasons why someone might become a cyberbully.

> The cyberbully wants revenge for harm that has been done to them. It is rarely the person they bully who has caused the harm.

> They turn their own unhappiness and insecurity on to someone else.

> They want other people to like and admire them.

> They are jealous of the person they bully.

> Online bullying allows the bully to be anonymous so they believe they can get away with their bullying.

> The cyberbully feels threatened by people who are different to themselves.

What should you do if you experience cyberbullying?

If you see someone being bullied

▶ Be careful not to join in. When you see a post that makes fun of someone, never click the 'like' button – not even as a joke. You will encourage the cyberbully and upset the person who the post is about.

▶ Say something positive about the person being bullied. Showing your support will make the bullying easier to bear.

▶ Offer support and friendship. Let the person talk if they need to. Encourage them to talk to an adult about the bullying.

If you are bullied

▶ Collect evidence. Take screenshots of posts so that you have a record even if the posts are deleted.

▶ Talk to someone you trust about the bullying. Talk to a friend, family member or teacher.

▶ Don't respond to the bullying. Responding can encourage the bully and make the situation worse.

▶ Spend some time offline.

 **Activity**

Write an information sheet on how to survive cyberbullying. If you have the time to do the Extra challenge, use some of the information you discover in your web search.

 Extra challenge

Search the internet to find one or more sites that give good information on how to deal with cyberbullying. Add the sites to your bookmark list.

✓ **Test**

1 List the actions you should take if you are bullied online.

2 Explain two methods that a cyberbully uses.

3 Explain why someone might decide to bully another person online.

4 What should you do if you receive a threatening message on your phone or computer?

2.5 Use content responsibly

In this lesson

You will learn:

▶ what intellectual property is

▶ how to use internet content responsibly and legally.

In this unit you have learned about the dangers posed by criminals on the internet. Theft of money and identity theft are serious problems on the internet. Another problem is the theft of intellectual property.

Intellectual property

Intellectual property means something that you have created using your mind (your intellect) and that you own.

Intellectual property can be:

▶ written work – books, poems, articles and web pages

▶ images and artwork – cartoons, paintings, photos and sculptures

▶ music and songs

▶ plans and designs

▶ computer software and games.

Intellectual property rights protect the creator of a piece of work. It is illegal for another person to steal or misuse the work. You can only use another person's work if they give you permission.

Copyright, trademarks and patents

There are different types of intellectual property. Each has its own symbol.

Type of intellectual property	Symbol	Description
Copyright	Ⓒ	**Copyright** means you have the right to copy your work. Other people must ask your permission before they can use it. You automatically have copyright for any work you create.
Trade mark	TM	Companies use trademarks to protect logos, slogans and product names. The Microsoft logo is a trademark.
Patent	Ⓟ	Inventors use patents to protect their new inventions. A patent stops other people from copying an invention and claiming it as their own idea.
Registered design	Ⓡ	This is used to protect designs like wallpaper and carpet patterns.

👓 Explore more

Every week, you use equipment and books at home and school. You use websites. You buy food and other items from shops. This week, look carefully at all the items you use and buy. Can you find an example of each of the four types of intellectual property described in the table?

What copyright means to you

You can legally use someone else's work in these situations:

▶ You have purchased their work. It may be an application program, game or music track. The work comes with a licence that allows you to use it. The licence will tell you exactly what you can and cannot do with the work.

▶ The owner of the work has given you permission to use their work. The owner will say what you can and cannot do with the content. For example, you may have permission to use a photo in your own work but not to change it.

Software piracy

Copyright theft is a type of cybercrime. Criminals make copies of music, games and films. They sell the copies, often over the internet. This type of crime is called piracy. When software is illegally copied and sold, it is called software piracy. When legal copies of software, music and games are sold, the person who created the work gets some money from each sale. When pirated copies are sold, the person does not get any money.

It is illegal to download and use pirated versions of software and other files.

⚙ Activity

Work with a partner or in a small group. Make a list of all the reasons why it might be a bad idea to download software from unofficial web pages.

Finding images on the internet

Many software apps provide images you can use – for example, web-editing tools like Wix and presentation software like Microsoft PowerPoint. You can also use many of the images that you find on the web.

Creative Commons

Many content owners make their images available free of charge on the internet. They use a special licence called **Creative Commons**. Creative Commons lets you use images without having to ask the owner for permission. Creative Commons music and video content is also available.

How to find Creative Commons images

There are websites that allow you to search for Creative Commons images. The one used in this example is called Wikimedia Commons. Other sites include Pixabay and Unsplash.

Enter key words for the images you are looking for in the search box. In this example the search is for 'Lions'. Your search will provide you with a list of images that match your key words. Sometimes you will see a page with information about the subject you have searched for. Scroll down the page to find the selection of images. Sometimes you will just see a list of links.

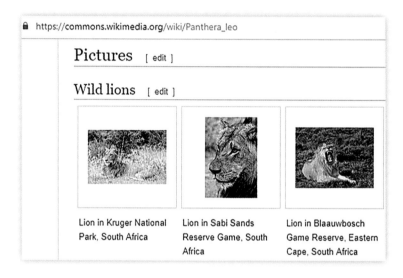

Clicking on an image opens a picture browser. The browser shows the image you have selected. There is information about the image below it.

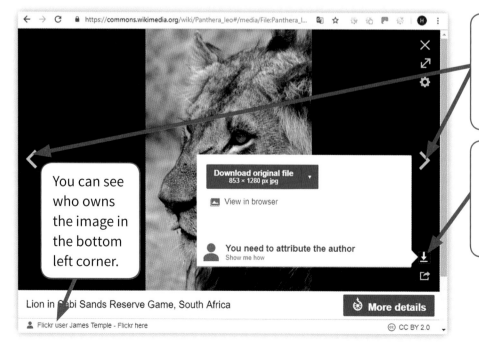

You can see who owns the image in the bottom left corner.

The arrows at the left and right of the page let you move between images without returning to the search list.

Click on the download button. The download box reminds you that you must attribute (credit) the author.

Giving credit for the images you use

The owner of a Creative Commons image gives you permission to use the image. Most owners ask you to give credit for the work. A credit includes the owner's name and a link to the website you got the image from.

Below the message 'You need to attribute the author' is a link that says 'Show me how'. If you click the link, the website provides a line of text that you can use as a credit when you use the image.

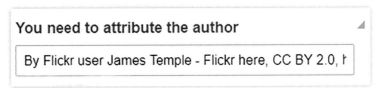

Choosing a graphics download site

Make sure you use a site you can trust when you search for Creative Commons files. Data files you download from the internet can contain malware. If you are unsure about a site, ask an adult for advice before you download any files.

 **Activity**

Search for an image of a tiger using Wikimedia Commons or another site that your teacher recommends. Download an image and add it to a word-processor document. Insert the credit provided by the website below the image.

 **Extra challenge**

Search the web to find out what the legal penalties are for software piracy. Penalties vary in different countries. You may need to add the name of your country in your search string.

 Test

1 Name two types of intellectual property.
2 What information should you use in a credit when you use someone else's work?
3 Explain why intellectual property theft and software piracy are bad for the owners of content.
4 Explain why it is a good idea to use a Creative Commons site when you are searching for images to use in your work.

2.6 Giving credit

In this lesson

You will learn:

▶ how to give credit when you use another person's work

▶ how to write a citation.

Using citations

How to credit an image

In the last lesson you learned how to find Creative Commons images on the web. Creative Commons images are shared by the people who made them. You can use most Creative Commons material free of charge, but you must give credit to the owner of the content. The text that you use to give credit is called a **citation** or an **attribution**.

In the lesson you downloaded an image from the Wikimedia Commons site. You learned how the site provides a citation for you to use with your downloaded image.

A Creative Commons citation includes the owner's name and a link to the image on the Wikimedia website. It looks like this:

> By Winfried Bruenken (Amrum) – Own work, CC BY-SA 2.5,
> https://commons.wikimedia.org/w/index.php?curid=1585973

Writing your own citation

Sometimes the owner of a piece of work does not provide a citation for you to use. In that case, you need to write your own citation. There are four pieces of information you should include in a citation:

▶ **author:** the name of the person who created the work

▶ **year:** when the work was produced

▶ **title:** for example, the title of an article you are quoting from or the title of a picture you want to use

▶ **internet address:** the address of the site you are taking the work from. If the work you are using does not come from the internet, use the title of the book or newspaper where you found the work.

 **Activity**

Can you find the four pieces of information you need for a citation in the news article at the top of the next page? Write a citation for this article.

There are times when you won't find some of the information you need. Don't worry. Just use what you can find.

How to use a citation in your work

You should add a citation for every piece of content you use that is not your own work. Adding a citation is straightforward:

▶ Type or paste the citation immediately below the image or quoted text.

▶ Use a font that is a little smaller than the main text in your document. For example, if the text in your document is 12 points, use 10 points for your citation.

Here is an example of a citation in a presentation slide:

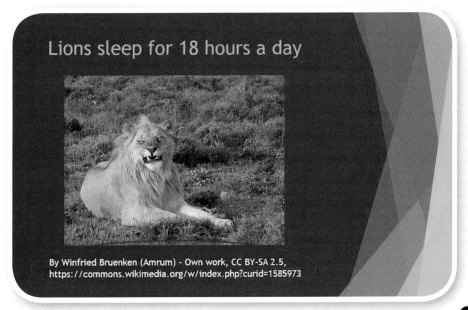

You can use the same method of adding a citation with other types of content. For example, you might use a video or a quote from a newspaper article. You might find a graph or a table that you want to use in your work. In every case, add a citation below the content.

Answer to the activity on page 54

A citation for the article shown at the top of page 55 will look like this:

Kaleem Shakil, 2019, Polar bears and snow leopards,
www.studentnewsonline.org

The citation includes the author's name, the year the article was written, the title of the article and the web address. Did you find all the information on the web page? If not, look at the image again to find the four parts of the citation.

Why are citations important?

There are four reasons why it is important to use citations to credit other people's work.

▶ You are giving credit to the person who created the content. Dishonest behaviour on the internet often involves someone losing money, for example by stealing someone's identity or their intellectual property. But people who create content are not just concerned with making money. People work hard to create new content and they are proud of it. They want to get credit for producing it.

▶ People use the internet to find information. They use web links from one document to another to find new facts. Someone who reads your work can follow the link in your citation to learn more about a subject.

▶ Citations make it clear what work is yours and what belongs to someone else. There is nothing wrong with using other people's knowledge in your own work. It is an important part of learning. But you must not pretend that someone else's work is your own. That is called **plagiarism**. If you use citations correctly, nobody can accuse you of plagiarism.

▶ Citations show your teacher that you have carried out research to complete your school assignments.

⏻ Digital citizen of the future

The internet can be dangerous. You can make it safer for yourself and others by doing the right things when you are online.

As a digital citizen of the future, remember to be cautious and to question everything you see and read on the internet. Keep your internet skills and knowledge up to date. Share your knowledge, and support friends and family who are learning how to use the internet.

Use the internet well and you will enjoy its benefits as you learn, work and lead your everyday life. Creating e-learning materials is a job that combines creative work with computing skills. Is it a career you would consider in the future?

⚙ Activity

Use word-processing or presentation software to create a short text about one of your hobbies or interests.

Write a paragraph about why you like this hobby or interest.

Find a relevant Creative Commons image to illustrate your text.

Search the web to find an interesting fact or quotation about your hobby or interest.

Add citations for the image and the quotation or interesting fact.

➦ Extra challenge

When you download images and videos from the web, you must be confident that the site you are downloading from is safe and that the content will be free from malware. In the last lesson, two alternative sites to Wikimedia Commons were mentioned: Pixabay and Unsplash. Choose one of these and search the web for reviews of your chosen site.

Test

1   Why is it a good idea to search for images on a Creative Commons website?
2   What must you do if you want to use another person's content in an assignment?
3   What is plagiarism?
4   How can using citations improve your work?

Check what you know

You have learned

▶ how to recognise the risks and dangers on the internet

▶ how to avoid risks and dangers on the internet

▶ how to use internet content responsibly.

Try the test and activities. They will help you to see how much you understand.

⚙ Activities

Create a guide for students called 'Protecting yourself online'. You can present your guide as a word-processed document, as a presentation with slides or as a series of web pages.

1 Say why it is important to protect yourself online.

2 Explain some risks people face online. You can include cyberbullying, malware or other risks you know about.

3 Add information about how people can protect themselves from risks online. For example, they can install anti-virus software and keep it up to date.

You can use the information in this unit and search online to find facts and images to illustrate your guide.

Remember to add citations for any quotations and images that you use.

Test

In this unit you have used websites. This test is about the websites you have used.

1   Think of one website that you have used to get information.

    a   Write down the name of the website.

    b   Write down one piece of information you got from this website.

2   Think of one online form that you have seen.

    a   Describe the online form.

    b   Write down one item of data collected by the online form.

3   What is a website cookie? What are cookies used for?

4   You can include information from a website in your work, but you must say where you got it from. Explain how to credit another person's work.

5   Explain how cookies can make websites easier to use.

6   Explain why intellectual property rights are important to a photographer.

Self-evaluation

- I answered test questions 1 and 2.

- I completed activity 1. I created a guide with reasons why it is important to protect yourself online.

- I answered test questions 1–4.

- I completed activities 1 and 2. I explained some of the risks people face online in my guide.

- I answered all the test questions.

- I completed all the activities. I described how people can protect themselves from risks online.

Re-read any parts of the unit you feel unsure about. Try the test and activities again – can you do more this time?

Computational thinking: Programming languages

You will learn

▶ how to make programs with Scratch and Python

▶ how to save commands as program files

▶ about the differences between programming languages

▶ what happens when the computer runs a program.

There are many different programming languages that programmers can use to create computer programs. In this unit you will write programs in two programming languages: Scratch and Python. You will look at programs made in Scratch. You will learn how to write programs in Python to do the same thing. You will discover how the two languages are different and how they are the same. You will also learn what happens when you run a computer program on your computer.

Previous books in this series have explored how to use the Scratch programming language.

Have you used Scratch before?

Yes
Write a description of the Scratch programs you have made.
What Scratch commands do you know? Write down as many as you can.

No
Prepare for this unit by finding out about Scratch. Read the previous books in this series to find out more.

Did you know?

Python and Scratch are both free to use. People who love programming developed these languages. The reason these languages are free is to encourage people to write programs.

A programmer called Guido van Rossum developed Python in 1991. Then lots of other programmers worked on Python to give it extra features. You can download your own copy of Python from the Python website.

Scratch was developed in 2003 at a University called MIT. A team of programmers worked together to make it. You can use Scratch on the Scratch website.

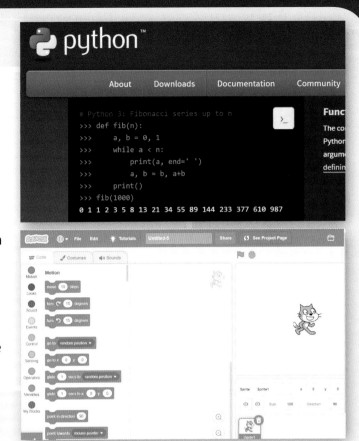

Talk about...

A program that is ready to use is **application software** – often called **app** for short. Do you have a smartphone with apps? Examples of smartphone apps include social media, messaging services, maps and games. What are your favourite smartphone apps? What new apps do you think might be invented in the future?

Python Shell

error message   machine code

IDE (Integrated Development Environment)

source code   compile

assign   string   interface

executable file

3.1 Make a simple calculator

In this lesson

You will learn:

▶ how to make a program interface

▶ how to use arithmetic operators.

Spiral back

In previous books you made programs using the Scratch programming language. In this lesson you will make a Scratch program. If you have not made programs in Scratch before, read the previous books in this series to learn how to use Scratch.

Program requirement

Before you plan and make a program you need to know what the program **requirement** is. The requirement tells you what the program must do. Here is an example requirement:

The user enters two numbers. The user selects an arithmetic operator (add, subtract, multiply or divide). The program outputs the result of the user's chosen calculation.

In this unit you will make a program that meets this requirement.

Arithmetic operators

Operators are symbols and terms used in programming. Operators are used to change values.

The program requirement above mentions **arithmetic operators**. These are operators that perform mathematical calculations: add, subtract, multiply and divide. In Scratch these operators are green blocks.

The four arithmetic operators are shown in the table. Almost all programming languages use the same symbols for these arithmetic operators.

Operator	What it does
+	add
-	subtract
*	multiply
/	divide

Operators

Algorithm

An **algorithm** is a plan to solve a problem. A programmer often starts planning their program by using a simpler version of the problem set out in the program requirement. They make an algorithm to solve the simpler problem. Later, they will add extra features to meet the full requirement.

This is the method that you will use in this lesson. Here is a simpler version of the problem in the program requirement:

Input two values and output the result of adding them together.

Start by making an algorithm to solve this simpler problem. The algorithm must set out the inputs and outputs of the program. It must also set out the processes that transform the inputs to create the required outputs.

```
input number 1
input number 2
result = number 1 + number 2
output the result
```

Create an interface

Every program has an **interface**. The interface is how the user interacts with the program. The interface allows the user to enter the inputs. The interface also provides the outputs.

Inputs to programs can include:

▶ touching a screen

▶ clicking with a mouse

▶ typing on a keyboard.

Outputs from programs can include:

▶ screen display, including words and colours

▶ sounds, including spoken words and sound effects

▶ movement of objects.

Create an interface in Scratch

Scratch makes it easy to create a colourful interface. Scratch programs control on-screen objects called sprites. You can use the sprites for both input and output.

▶ **Getting inputs:** You can make the sprite ask a question in a speech bubble. A box appears for the user input.

▶ **Showing outputs:** You can make the sprite say outputs in speech bubbles.

Here is a Scratch interface with a sprite and a colourful backdrop.

enter a number

 **Activity**

Begin a program interface in Scratch like the one shown here. Choose one sprite and a backdrop. Do not make the program yet. You will make the program in the next activity.

Create variables

Variables store values. Scratch provides two ready-made variables:

▶ 'answer': This variable will store the user's input.

▶ 'my variable': This is a general-purpose variable. It can store any value.

You can make variables with better names than 'my variable'. Use names that remind you what value each variable will store.

Look at the algorithm on page 63. Three variables are mentioned in the algorithm:

▶ 'number 1'   ▶ 'number 2'   ▶ 'result'.

Create these variables in the Scratch program.

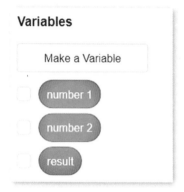

You will not use 'my variable' in your program. If you wish, you can right-click on this variable and delete it.

Starting event

The first block in a Scratch program must be an 'Event' block. The event on this block will make the program start. Here are some 'Event' blocks.

Your program will start when the user clicks on the sprite. Find the 'Event' block that says 'when this sprite clicked'. Drag the block into the script area at the centre of the screen. Now you have set the starting event for your program.

Make the program

Now you will add more blocks to the 'Event' block. You will need Scratch programming skills. You need to know how to:

▶ use the 'ask' block to get user input

▶ set the value of a variable

▶ use 'Operator' blocks

▶ use the 'say' block to show output.

All of these skills are covered in earlier books in this series.

Here is the completed program.

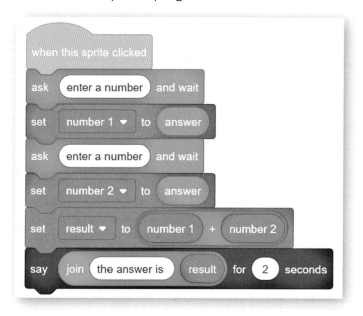

![Activity]

Make a program to do an addition calculation. Use the blocks shown in the image of the completed program. Run your program to check that it works.

![Extra challenge]

Extend your program so that it does other calculations.

Add three more sprites to the interface. Program each sprite to do a different calculation: addition, subtraction, multiplication, division.

Add commands so that each sprite tells you what calculation it can do.

![Be creative]

The Scratch interface provides many ready-made backdrops and sprites.

You can also upload a picture file to the interface to use as a backdrop or sprite.

Here are some ideas to create a customised and personalised Scratch program.

▶ Assemble a ready-made Scratch backdrop and sprites to create an original design.

▶ Search online for suitable images to use as a backdrop or sprite.

▶ Make your own images, for example, using graphics software.

![Test]

1 What are the four arithmetic operators?

2 What is an interface?

3 An algorithm sets out the inputs and outputs of a program. What else does it set out?

4 When you make a Scratch program, what is the purpose of the 'Event' block?

In this lesson

You will learn:

▶ how to use the Python programming language for input and output

▶ how to make a variable and give it a value.

Programming languages

When you make a computer program you use a programming language. In the last lesson you used the Scratch programming language. Scratch is a block-based programming language. Each block stands for a command. To make programs, you fit blocks together.

Here is a very simple Scratch program. It includes input and output commands.

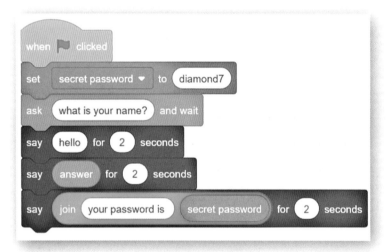

What does this program do? If you are not sure, make the program and run it to check.

Python

Python is a text-based programming language. The commands in Python are text. To make Python carry out a command you must type the command.

In this lesson you will enter Python commands that match the Scratch program shown above.

The Python Shell

When you start Python, a window opens. This is called the **Python Shell**. You can enter Python commands one at a time into the Python Shell. When you have typed a command, press the 'Enter' key. Python will carry out the command.

```
Python 3.7.1 Shell                                          –  □  ×
File  Edit  Shell  Debug  Options  Window  Help
Python 3.7.1 (v3.7.1:260ec2c36a, Oct 20 201
8, 14:57:15) [MSC v.1915 64 bit (AMD64)] on
win32
Type "help", "copyright", "credits" or "lic
ense()" for more information.
>>> |
                                                        Ln: 3  Col: 4
```

Using variables

Look at the first command in the Scratch program. It sets the variable 'secret password' to the value 'diamond7'.

Now you will do the same thing in Python.

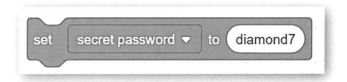

Naming variables in Python

Just as you did in Scratch, choose meaningful variable names. The variable name should remind you what value is stored in the variable. There are rules in Python about naming variables. A variable name must:

▶ be one word only – no spaces

▶ use only letters, numbers and the underscore character

▶ start with a letter.

In Scratch the variable is called 'secret password'. In Python we must use a single word, for example, `password`.

Setting the value of a variable

In Python, you make a variable and set its value with a single command. The command to make a variable and set its value has this structure:

```
variable = value
```

Enter the name of the variable, then an equals sign, then the value. For example:

```
password = "diamond7"
```

This will make a variable called `password` and give it the value `"diamond7"`.

Get input

The next section of the Scratch program asks the user to input their name. To get user input in Scratch you use the light blue 'ask' block. User input is stored as a ready-made variable called 'answer':

To get user input in Python you use the command `input`. The following Python command will get user input and store it as a variable called `name`:

```
name = input("what is your name? ")
```

The text inside the brackets is called the prompt. The prompt tells the user what to input. Can you see that the prompt includes a space after the question mark? That means there will be space between the text and the user's input. You use a space like this in Scratch too.

Show output

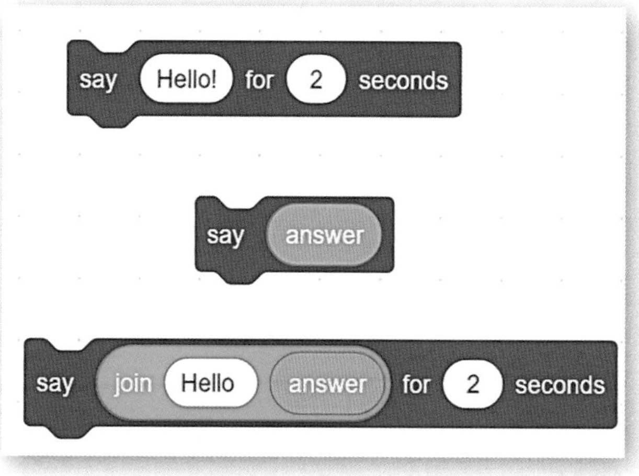

The final part of the Scratch program shows the program output. To produce output in Scratch you use a 'say' block. Whatever you put into a 'say' block will be output in a speech bubble.

To produce output in Python you use the command `print`. After this command you insert brackets. Whatever you put inside the brackets will be output. For example, you might want to output:

▶ a number or calculation

▶ a string (that means some text in quote marks)

▶ the name of a variable.

Here are some commands. Enter them one at a time into the Python Shell and see the result of each command.

```
password = "diamond7"

name = input("what is your name? ")

print("hello")

print(name)

print("your password is", password)
```

The picture on the right shows the output. The Python Shell carries out each command in turn.

```
>>> password = "diamond7"
>>> name = input("what is your name? ")
what is your name? Mia
>>> print("hello")
hello
>>> print(name)
Mia
>>> print("your password is", password)
your password is diamond7
>>>
```

Program errors

A programmer using Python must enter each command using exactly the right text. Then the computer can recognise the command. If you make a mistake when you type the command, the computer will not recognise the command. You will see an **error message**.

Mistakes you might make

Here are some examples of errors you could make when you type a Python command. You might:

▶ spell a word incorrectly

▶ put the words in the wrong order

▶ use a capital letter instead of a lower-case letter

▶ leave out brackets or other symbols.

Error message

It is easy to make mistakes when you type a command. For example, in this command the programmer typed `Print` instead of `print`.

```
>>> Print("Hello")
Traceback (most recent call last):
  File "<pyshell#7>", line 1, in <module>
    Print("Hello")
NameError: name 'Print' is not defined
```

If you make a mistake, the Python Shell displays an error message. An error message tells you that there is a mistake. The error message helps you to find the error. Then you can type the command again, but without the error.

Remember: It is OK to make mistakes. Even the best programmers make mistakes. Make sure you read the error message and fix the error. Then your programs will always work the way you want.

 **Activity**

Use the Python Shell to enter all the commands shown in this lesson, one after the other.

Extra challenge

Here is another Scratch program. Enter commands into the Python Shell that match this program.

 Test

1 Write the Python command to make a variable called `city` with the value `"Paris"`.

2 Write the Python command to output the variable `age`.

3 Write the Python command to ask the user `"How old are you?"`, get user input, and store the user input as the variable `age`.

4 Explain how error messages help you to be a good programmer.

In this lesson

You will learn:

▶ how to save commands into a program file

▶ how to run a program you have made.

Save Python commands as a program

In the last lesson, you entered Python commands in the Python Shell. The Python Shell carries out the commands right away.

But the Python Shell does not save the commands. If you want to use the same commands again, you have to type them again. This is more work for you and there is a chance you will make a typing mistake.

Most programmers save their commands. Saving commands in a file makes a Python program. Then you can reuse the commands as often as you want with no extra work.

In this lesson you will learn how to save your commands.

Create a file

In the Python Shell, open the 'File' menu. Choose 'New File'.

A new window will open on the screen. Now there are two open windows. One is the Python Shell. The other is the file window. The file window is empty.

File	Edit	Shell	Debug	Options
New File			Ctrl+N	
Open...			Ctrl+O	
Open Module...			Alt+M	
Recent Files				▶

Enter commands

Now type in all the commands from the last lesson, one after the other. Each command goes on a separate line.

The computer does not carry out the commands yet.

```
password = "diamond7"
name = input("what is your name? ")
print("hello")
print(name)
print("your password is", password)
```

Colours in the Python program

You will notice that the commands you have typed are shown in different colours on the screen.

▶ Names of variables are shown in black.

▶ Symbols such as commas and brackets are shown in black.

▶ Input and print functions are shown in purple.

▶ Text strings are shown in green.

You will learn some other colours later.

Find errors

Pay attention to the colour of the commands you type. That will help you find errors in your commands.

For example, a student wanted to enter the command to output the word "Hello" on the screen. This is what he typed:

```
Print(hello)
```

There are two mistakes in this command.

▶ Print should be lower case (no capital letter): `print`

▶ Hello should be inside quote marks: `"hello"`

Find this command in your program. Change it to include these errors. Look carefully at the colours in this command.

`Print(hello)` ◀— The colours have gone from the command. The whole line is in black text.

The colour of the text shows you that the words are typed incorrectly. The word `print` should be purple. The word `"hello"` should be green. Now you have found the error you can fix it by typing the word correctly.

`print("hello")` ◀— When you correct the errors, the text changes to the correct colours.

Save

Now you have entered all the commands. You can save the file. Open the 'File' menu and choose 'Save'. Type a name for your program, for example, 'practice program 1', but you can use any name.

Run the program

Now you have made a Python program. Next you will **run** the program. When you run a program, the computer will carry out all the commands stored in the program.

Find the 'Run' menu at the top of the file window. Click on 'Run Module'.

All the outputs of the program appear in the Python Shell window. Type your response to the question. Each command is carried out, one after the other.

Error messages

In the last lesson you learned that programmers sometimes make mistakes. A simple typing error can stop your program working. Text colour can help you to find errors before you run the program.

But sometimes errors remain when you run the program. That is OK. Python will find the mistake. It will stop the program and show you an error message. Python's error message will help you to work out what the error is.

Error messages in the Python Shell window

A student ran a program with this line:

```
print(hello)
```

This error message appeared in the Python Shell window:

```
Traceback (most recent call last):
  File "C:/Python/practice program 1.py", line 2
    print(hello)
NameError: name 'hello' is not defined
```

The error message says `NameError: name 'hello' is not defined`. This tells you that the computer thinks `hello` is the name of something, for example, a variable. The computer does not recognise that `hello` is a text string, because it does not have quote marks.

Error messages in the file window

Another student made a different error. He forgot to put in the second set of quote marks at the end of the line.

```
print("hello)
```

This error message appeared in the program file window.

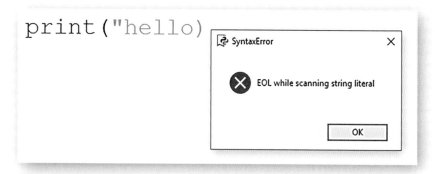

This error message is displayed in a different way. It appears in a little window on the screen. The error message says 'EOL while scanning string literal'. EOL stands for 'End Of Line'. The computer is saying it reached the end of the line before it reached the end of the text string. That tells the student that he must enter quote marks to close the text string.

Look out for error messages and fix the errors that you see. You will learn more about finding and removing program errors in Unit 4 of this book.

Integrated Development Environment (IDE)

The software that you use to write and run programs is called an **IDE**. That stands for **Integrated Development Environment**. An IDE lets you enter and save program commands. It displays error messages. It runs the program. It lets the user enter the input and it shows the output.

- Scratch is a colourful block-based programming language. The IDE for Scratch is a web page. There is an area to make the program, and there is a 'stage' area where you see the program display.

- The IDE you are using to make Python programs is called IDLE. It is simple text-based software. It allows you to make and save programs. The program output is shown in the Python Shell.

 **Activity**

Make the Python program shown in this lesson. Save and run the program. Correct any errors.

Extra challenge

Here is a Scratch program. Make a Python program to match this program. Save and run the program.

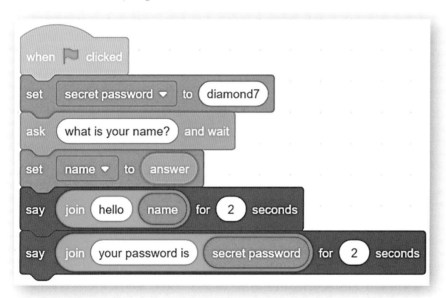

 Test

1. What is the advantage of making a program file instead of typing commands in the Python Shell?

2. Name two different colours used in the Python program file window. Name the type of program content that has each colour.

3. Explain two different ways you can find errors in your Python programs.

4. Describe one difference between the IDE for Scratch and the IDE for Python.

In this lesson

You will learn:

▶ some different data types

▶ how to change data type

▶ how to do calculations in Python.

Use Scratch

Here is a simple Scratch program.

This program has three variables called 'number 1', 'number 2' and 'total'. The program has commands that:

▶ set the values of 'number 1' and 'number 2'

▶ set the value of 'total' as 'number 1' + 'number 2'

▶ output the variable 'total'.

You will enter commands in the Python Shell to carry out the same task as this Scratch program.

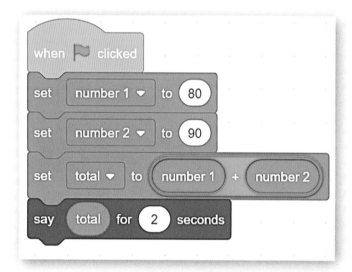

Use the Python Shell

You will make variables to store the number values. Enter this command in the Python Shell:

```
number1 = 80
```

This command makes the variable `number1`. It also **assigns** the value `80` to this variable. Assigning a value to a variable is the same as setting the value of the variable.

Now enter this command. Can you explain what it does?

```
number2 = 90
```

Next enter this command:

```
total = number1 + number2
```

This command creates the variable `total`. It assigns a value to `total`. The value is `number1` plus `number2`. You can see that Python uses the same arithmetic operators as Scratch.

Finally, output the result:

```
print(total)
```

Press 'Enter' to see the correct output on the screen.

Input values in Scratch

Here is a new Scratch program. This program asks the user to input two values. The program stores the input values as 'number 1' and 'number 2'. Then the program outputs the total.

If you have time, make this program in Scratch. Run the program and check that it produces the correct result.

Input values in Python

Lena wanted to do the same task using Python. She used the Python Shell to test the commands. Lena knew the correct Python command to go first. This command assigns user input to a variable called `number1`.

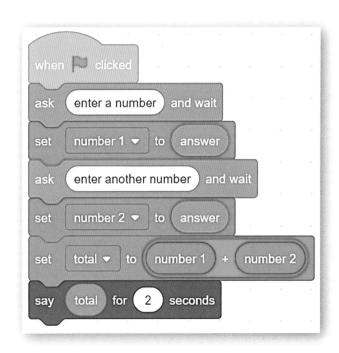

```
number1 = input("enter a number ")
```

Here is the Python Shell with all the commands that Lena entered. If you have time, do this activity for yourself.

```
>>> number1 = input("enter a number ")
enter a number 80
>>> number2 = input("enter a number ")
enter a number 90
>>> total = number1 + number2
>>> print(total)
8090
```

There was no error message, but Lena did not get the correct result. She entered 80 and 90. Python output the result 8090. Instead of adding the two numbers, Python has joined them together. But why?

To understand why this happened, you need to know about data types.

Data types

In Unit 1, you learned how a computer stores data in its memory. A computer stores all data using a digital code. For example, text characters are stored using ASCII code. Python has different data types:

▶ ASCII characters are stored as **string** data type.

▶ Whole numbers are stored as **integer** data type.

▶ Numbers with a decimal point are stored as **float** data type.

String data

String data can include any keyboard characters. The characters of the string are shown inside quote marks. You can use double or single quote marks.

Here are some examples of strings.

```
"hello"

"I am 99 years old"

"99"
```

Some strings are made of digits. They look like numbers. But they are not number values. String data cannot be used in calculations. Only integer and float data can be used in calculations.

Input data

In Python, user input is stored as a string. Can you spot the problem?

▶ Input data is stored as a string.

▶ Strings cannot be used in calculations.

Now you know why Lena's program did not work. The two variables `number1` and `number2` are string values. They are not number values. The add sign joins the strings together instead of adding them.

Change Data Type

Convert to integer

A Python function called `int` converts any variable to integer data type. The command looks like this:

```
variable = int(variable)
```

Lena used this function. She converted `number1` and `number2` to integer data type:

```
number1 = int(number1)

number2 = int(number2)
```

The image shows all Lena's commands in the Python Shell. This time she got the correct result.

Try it for yourself.

```
>>> number1 = input("enter a number ")
enter a number 80
>>> number1 = int(number1)
>>> number2 = input("enter a number ")
enter a number 90
>>> number2 = int(number2)
>>> total = number1 + number2
>>> print(total)
170
```

Convert to other data types

The command to convert a variable to float data type looks like this:

```
variable = float(variable)
```

The command to convert to string data type looks like this:

```
variable = str(variable)
```

But do not type the word 'variable' in your commands. Type the name of the variable you want to change.

Make a Python program

So far, Lena has entered all the commands using the Python Shell. She has checked that they work.

Next she typed all the commands in the file window to make a Python program file.

```python
number1 = input("enter a number ")
number1 = int(number1)
number2 = input("enter a number ")
number2 = int(number2)
total = number1 + number2
print(total)
```

She saved the file. Then she ran the file. The Python program worked.

Summary

A Python program to add two numbers together needs these commands:

▶ Get input from the user and store it as a variable called `number1`.

▶ Get input from the user and store it as a variable called `number2`.

▶ Convert both variables to integer data type.

▶ Make a variable called `total` with the value `number1` + `number2`.

▶ Print out `total`.

If you use the float data type instead of integer data type, you can add numbers with a decimal point.

 **Activity**

Make a Python program to input two integers, add them together and output the total. Check for errors and fix them. Save your work.

 **Extra challenge**

You have learned that the arithmetic operators will not do calculations with string data. So what do the arithmetic operators do with string variables? Try these commands in the Python Shell.

```python
print("a" + "b")
print("a" * 9)
```

What have you found out about the arithmetic operators and strings?

▶ Write a Python command to draw a line of 35 dashes across the screen.

▶ Make a Python program. Ask the user to input a value. Output the number of dashes that the user has entered.

 Test

1 Write the Python command to assign the value `9.99` to a variable called `price`.

2 What is the data type of the `price` variable?

3 The variable `points` stores data that the user has input. What is the data type of this variable?

4 Write a command to convert the `points` variable to any numerical data type (integer or float).

In this lesson

You will learn:

▶ how to choose the best programming language for a task.

Programming languages

In this unit you have made programs using Scratch and Python. Scratch and Python are **programming languages**. Programmers use programming languages to write working programs.

There are lots of other programming languages. Here are some examples:

▶ Java   ▶ C++   ▶ Visual Basic.

Which programming language is best? Every programmer has their favourite. Different programmers recommend different languages. The best programming language to use depends on the task you have to do. In this lesson you will look at how to choose the best programming language for a task.

Compare programming languages

Before you can choose the best programming language to use, you need to compare the languages. Think about the good points and bad points of each language.

 **Activity**

You know two programming languages – Scratch and Python. Here are some features of Scratch and Python.

A Programs take up a lot of space on the screen.

B You can enter a lot of program commands in a small space.

C Programs are made by combining visual elements.

D It is easy to make a lively user interface with colourful images.

E Programs have variables.

F Programs have arithmetic operators.

G Programs have input and output.

H The program elements are blocks.

I The program elements are text only.

J If there are errors, the programs will not work, or they will do the wrong thing.

K You must convert user input to a numerical data type before you do a calculation.

L There is no need to convert user input to a numerical data type before you do a calculation.

Sort the features in the boxes into three groups. Copy and complete the table.

Features of Scratch only	Features of Python only	Features of both languages

Why choose Scratch?

It is easy to understand why many teachers choose Scratch to use with their students. Scratch shares important features with other programming languages, such as:

▶ variables

▶ operators

▶ input and output

▶ structures such as loops.

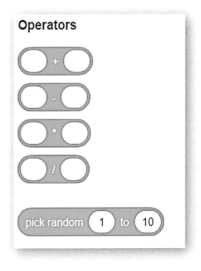

Scratch also has special features which make it suitable for learners. For example:

▶ It is easy to make a working program by fitting blocks together.

▶ You don't need to type the commands, so you make fewer errors.

▶ Your programs have a lively user interface with sprites and a backdrop.

▶ There is no need to convert between data types.

These features make Scratch very good for young learners. Using Scratch helps students develop their programming skills.

Why choose Python?

When students become more confident at programming, they often move to a text-based language such as Python. Python does not have a lively block-based interface like Scratch. But Python has some important advantages that Scratch does not have. For example:

▶ Text commands take up much less space on the screen than block commands.

▶ Python has many more operators and other processing features.

▶ It is easier to write long complex programs in Python than in Scratch.

For these reasons, professional programmers use Python much more than Scratch to make programs that are used in real life.

Apps made using Python

Professional programmers often use a mixture of different languages to make their programs. These well-known apps were partly made using Python and partly using other languages:

▶ YouTube

▶ Dropbox

▶ Google

▶ Netflix.

Versions of these well-known computer games were made using Python:

▶ Civilization

▶ The Sims

▶ Toontown Online.

Python is one of the top five programming languages used in the world today.

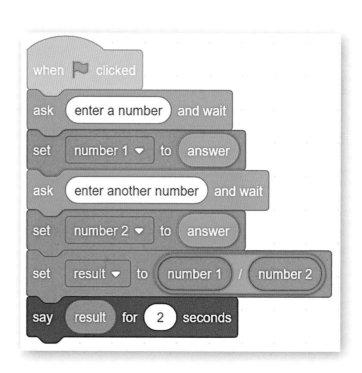

Easy to learn and use

You have to pay to use some programming languages. But Scratch and Python are free to use.

▶ You use Scratch on a free website.

▶ You can download Python to your computer. Download means copy from a website to your own computer.

Both Scratch and Python have friendly communities. They provide lots of help for a new programmer.

▶ There are online tutorials.

▶ There are examples of programs to look at.

▶ There are forums where you can ask questions and people will give you advice.

These advantages make both Scratch and Python good languages for new learners.

Example – division

Now you will make a program to meet this requirement:

The user enters two numbers. The program outputs the result of dividing the first number by the second.

Here is a version of this program created using Scratch.

```
when 🏳 clicked
ask  enter a number  and wait
set  number 1 ▾  to  answer
ask  enter another number  and wait
set  number 2 ▾  to  answer
set  result ▾  to  ( number 1 / number 2 )
say  result  for  2  seconds
```

 **Activity**

Here are the commands used in the Scratch program shown above.

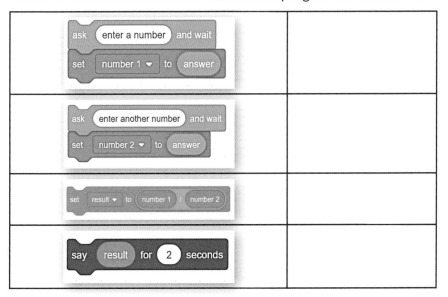

ask enter a number *and wait* / *set* number 1 *to* answer	
ask enter another number *and wait* / *set* number 2 *to* answer	
set result *to* number 1 / number 2	
say result *for* 2 *seconds*	

1 Copy this table into your book. Next to the Scratch command blocks write the matching Python command. Sometimes you will need to write more than one command.

2 Write the complete Python program to match the Scratch program.

 **Extra challenge**

1 Write a Scratch program that:
  ▶ asks the user to input two numbers
  ▶ stores the numbers as variables 'x' and 'y'
  ▶ outputs the result of 'x% of y'.

2 Write a Python program to match the Scratch program you have made.

 **Digital citizen of the future**

If you want to be a programmer when you grow up, you need to learn to write programs in a text-based language such as Python. When you are confident with Python, try to learn another text-based language.

Explore more

If you can, visit the Python website. Follow the instructions to download Python to your computer at home. Now you can make Python programs at home.

 Test

1 Name one programming language you have learned and one programming language you have not learned.

2 Name one good feature that Scratch shares with Python.

3 Name one good feature of Scratch that Python does not have. Explain how this feature helps young learners to make programs in Scratch.

4 You can buy apps made using Python. But you cannot buy many apps made using Scratch. In your own words, explain why.

3.6 Source code and machine code

In this lesson

You will learn:

▶ how the computer runs a program

▶ how source code is turned into machine code.

Machine code

In the last lesson you learned that many different programming languages are available. But what language does the computer use?

The computer uses a language called **machine code**. Machine code is the only language the computer can understand. Machine code is made entirely of numbers. Every computer action has its own number in machine code. The computer reads the code and then does the action.

Machine code is very hard for a human programmer to read and write. It has no words or names or operators – just lots and lots of numbers.

Executable file

Some of the files on your computer are made of machine code. A file made of machine code is called an **executable file**. Execute means carry out a command. An executable file is a file with commands that the computer can carry out.

All the software on your computer is made of executable code. Remember that software that you use for a particular task is called application software – often called app for short. When your computer runs an app, it carries out all the commands in the executable file.

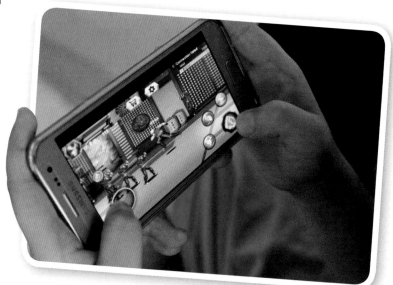

For example, Raj has a computer game on his smartphone. When he runs the app, the computer processor in his phone executes the machine code instructions. That makes the game happen on the screen of his smartphone.

Source code

Programmers don't usually write programs using machine code. They use other programming languages instead. Python and Scratch are examples of programming languages.

A set of commands that a programmer writes in a programming language is called **source code**.

But there is a problem. The computer can only understand machine code. The commands have to be converted from the programming language into machine code. Then the computer can understand the commands. Converting a program from a programming language to machine code is called **translating** the program.

 **Activity**

Here are some descriptions of source code and of machine code.

> **A** It is made of numbers.

> **B** The computer can execute this code.

> **C** It has to be translated before the computer can understand it.

> **D** It is easy for a human programmer to understand.

> **E** The computer can understand this code.

> **F** It is written in a programming language.

> **G** The computer can run this file without translating it.

> **H** A software app is made of this code.

> **I** When you write a program, you make this type of file.

> **J** A Python program is this type of code.

Sort the features in the boxes into two groups. Copy and complete the table.

Source code	Machine code

Compiling

The process of turning a program into an executable file is called **compiling**. To compile a program you need a piece of software called a **compiler**.

Andy is a professional programmer. He has an idea for a game app. These are the steps he follows to create his app:

▶ He plans the algorithm for the app.

▶ He writes the program in a programming language.

▶ He uses a compiler to turn the program into an executable file.

At the end of this process, Andy has an executable file. He can sell the executable file. The executable file is made of machine code. Anyone who buys the file can run the app. Then they can play the game that Andy made.

Interpreting

There is another way to translate source code into machine code. This method is called **interpreting**.

Interpreting works like this:

▶ The computer reads one command from the program.

▶ The computer translates and executes the command right away.

▶ The computer moves on to the next command.

When a program is interpreted, the computer does not store any machine code. You only have the source code. Every time you run the program, the computer has to translate the source code into machine code again.

Scratch

When you use Scratch you work on the Scratch website. You make and run the program in your web browser. Every web browser has an interpreter built into it. The interpreter understands a language called **JavaScript**. Scratch programs can run inside your browser using the JavaScript interpreter.

Python

There are different ways to use Python. The standard version you used in this unit is interpreted. The Python interpreter converts Python commands into machine code that the computer understands. The Python interpreter is part of the software that you put onto your computer when you install Python.

See for yourself

This Python program inputs two numbers and multiplies them together. It has a mistake in it. Can you spot it?

```
number1 = input("enter a number ")
number1 = int(number1)
number2 = inpt("enter a number")
number2 = int(number2)
result = number1 * number2
print(result)
```

This is what happens when you run this program:

▶ Lines 1 and 2 have no mistakes. The computer interprets and runs these commands.

▶ Line 3 has a mistake. The computer stops. It cannot interpret this command. You will see an error message.

```
enter a number 70
Traceback (most recent call last):
  File "C:\Python\temp.py", line 3,
    number2 = inpt("enter a number")
NameError: name 'inpt' is not defined
```

 **Activity**

Write a Python program which:

▶ asks the user to input three numbers

▶ multiplies the three numbers together

▶ outputs the result.

 **Extra challenge**

Use Scratch to write a quiz program. The sprite asks the user a question about source code and machine code. The program tells the user if their answer is right or wrong.

If you have time, add more questions to the quiz program.

 Test

1 Programmers don't usually write programs using machine code. Why not?

2 What is an executable file?

3 Why does source code need to be translated before the computer can execute it?

4 How is Scratch code translated into commands that the computer can understand?

Check what you know

You have learned

▶ how to make programs with Scratch and Python

▶ how to save commands as program files

▶ about the differences between programming languages

▶ what happens when the computer runs a program.

Try the test and activities. They will help you to see how much you understand.

Test

Louis uses a wheelchair to travel around his city. Some roads in the city have steps so he cannot use these roads in his wheelchair. When Louis was a student, he made an app that finds a wheelchair-accessible route to any place in the city. He shared the app with other people who use wheelchairs. People who use pushchairs and buggies found the app useful too.

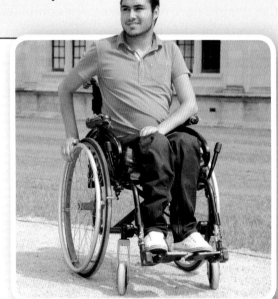

When he left university, Louis became a professional programmer.

People can download Louis's app. Then they can run the app.

1 Explain what 'download' means.

2 Explain what 'run' means.

Louis wrote his app using source code. The source code was translated into machine code.

3 Why did the source code have to be translated into machine code?

4 Why didn't Louis write the app in machine code?

5 Identify one way of translating source code into machine code.

6 Imagine you want to make a similar app for wheelchair users in your city. Will you use Python or Scratch to make the app? Give reasons for your choice.

⚙ Activities

Ritu has made a program to create new passwords. The program asks for the user's name and their favourite colour. The program makes a password by joining the two user inputs.

First Ritu made the program in Scratch.

Then Ritu made the program in Python.

1 Make the Scratch program shown here.

2 Make a Python program that asks the user for their name and their favourite colour.

3 Extend the Python program to make a password from `name + colour`. Print the password.

4 Change the Python program so that the password is the user's favourite colour × 2. For example, if the user's favourite colour is gold, their password will be 'goldgold'.

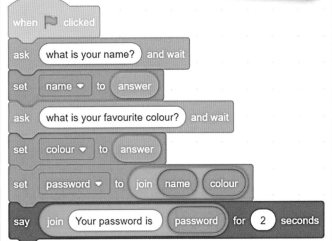

Self-evaluation

- I answered test questions 1 and 2.
- I completed activity 1. I made a program in Scratch.
- I started the Python program.
- I answered test questions 1–4.
- I completed activities 1 and 2. I made a Scratch program and a Python program that worked.
- I answered all the test questions.
- I completed activities 1–4. I completed all the programs.

Re-read any parts of the unit you feel unsure about. Try the test and activities again – can you do more this time?

4 Programming: It all adds up

You will learn

▶ how to use conditional (if) structures in Python

▶ how to make Python programs with loops

▶ how to find and fix errors in programs

▶ how to make your programs user friendly and readable.

In this unit you will make a program which adds up the number of birds visiting a bird feeder. This program will be useful for scientists and nature reporters. As you work through the lessons in this unit you will make the program. You will use programming structures such as loops and 'if… else'. You will learn to read error messages and to improve your program by removing errors.

 **Unplugged**

Work in a group of four. In this activity you will act out a computer program.

Write numbers on slips of paper and put them in a box or other container. You can write any numbers you like. Make sure at least one of the numbers is 0 (zero). You also need a blank piece of paper and a pen.

Team roles: Each person in the team will play the role of part of the program. There are four roles:

▶ Program

▶ Total

▶ Input

▶ Logical test.

The person who is the 'Program' reads out the instructions on the next page, one at a time. As 'Program' reads each instruction, they point to the person named. That person then carries out the instruction. If the person who is the 'Logical test' shouts "Stop!", the program stops.

Instructions:

1. **Total:** record the value 0.
2. **Input:** take a number from the box and read it out.
3. **Logical test:** shout "Stop!" if you hear the number zero.
4. **Total:** add the input number to 'total'.
5. **Program:** go back to line 2 and continue from there.

When the program stops, check the value of 'total'. That is the final output of the program.

Logical test

Program

Input

Total

Did you know?

The software you make in this unit will count the number of bird visitors. But you might also want to know what types of birds the visitors are. You can download apps onto your phone that help you identify bird species. Some apps ask you a few questions about the bird (size, colour, etc.). You input the answers and the app outputs photos of possible bird species. Other apps, such as ChirpOMatic, accept sound input. You input a sound recording of birdsong and the app outputs the name of the species.

Talk about...

In this unit you will make a program to record the number of bird visitors to a bird feeder. Helping scientists to study nature is one way that computers can help protect the environment. Overall, do you think computers have had a positive or negative impact on nature? Think of as many examples as you can on both sides of the debate.

conditional structure

logical test   indent   for loop

while loop   syntax error

logical error   user friendly

interface   readable

In this lesson

You will learn:

▶ how to create an 'if' structure in Python and Scratch

▶ how to make logical tests with relational operators.

Conditional structure

In Unit 3 you created a Scratch program that added two numbers together. The program always did the same thing. Now you will adapt the program so that it can add or subtract. The user's choice will change what it does.

To vary what a program does, you use a **conditional structure**. This type of structure is also called an 'if' structure. The structure begins with the word 'if' and then has a **logical test**. The commands inside the if structure are only carried out if the test is True.

Logical test

The result of a logical test can be True or False. A logical test usually compares two values. It uses a relational operator to compare the two values.

Relational operators

In Scratch the relational operators are three green blocks.

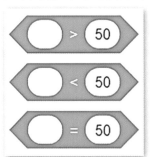

The table shows the meaning of the three relational operators in Scratch.

Operator	What it means
>	greater than
<	less than
=	equal to

Spiral back

In previous books you made programs using the 'if… else' block in Scratch. Actions inside the 'if… else' block are controlled by a logical test. In this lesson you will make programs in Scratch and Python using the 'if… else' structure. Look back at previous books to refresh your understanding of Scratch.

Comparing values

To make a logical test you compare two values. The comparison can be either True or False. Here is an example:

4 > 8

This means '4 is greater than 8'. This comparison is FALSE, so the logical test has the value False.

Here is another one.

3 + 4 = 7

This means '3 plus 4 is equal to 7'. This comparison is TRUE so the logical test has the value True.

 **Activity**

Here are some examples of logical tests. One of the values is missing. Copy the logical tests into your book and fill in a missing value that makes each test True.

a (7 * 6) < ☐   **c** 400 / 50 > ☐   **e** 12.34 = ☐

b 23 + 3 = ☐   **d** 99.999 < ☐

Make a Scratch program

Here is an example of a Scratch program that includes a conditional structure.

The user has to choose whether to add two numbers. If the user types 'Y', the program will add the numbers. This program includes the conditional 'if' block.

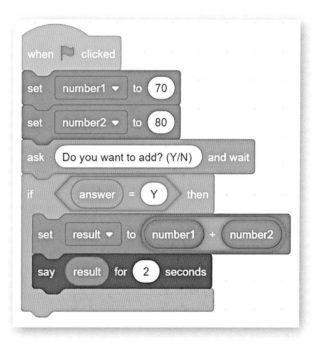

This block starts with the logical test:

'answer = Y'

If the user enters the letter 'Y', the test is True. The computer carries out the commands inside the 'if' block. If the user does not enter the letter 'Y', the test is False. The computer does not carry out any commands.

 **Activity**

Make the Scratch program shown in the image above. Run the program to see what happens when you enter 'Y' and when you enter anything else.

Make a Python program

Now you will make the same program using Python. You can use 'if… else' structures in Python programs. But Python does not use blocks. Instead you type the commands as text.

Set variables

The Scratch program has three variables: 'number1', 'number2' and 'answer'. The values of 'number1' and 'number2' are set in the program. The user inputs the value of 'answer'.

You already know how to do these commands in Python:

```
number1 = 70

number2 = 80

answer = input("do you want to add? (Y/N) ")
```

Make the logical test

Python has more relational operators than Scratch. Here are the main relational operators that you might use.

For this program you will use the 'equal to' operator. The logical test compares the user answer to the text string 'Y'. If they match, the test is True.

```
if answer == "Y"
```

Operator	What it means
==	equal to
!=	not equal to
>	greater than
<	less than
>=	greater than or equal to
<=	less than or equal to

Inside the conditional structure

Now you must put commands inside the conditional structure. The computer will carry out these commands if the test is True.

```
if answer == "Y":
```
← Put a colon (:) at the end of the logical test.

All the commands that follow the colon will be **indented**. That means they will be set in from the left of the file window.

```
if answer == "Y":

    result = number1 + number2

    print(result)
```

The computer will only carry out the indented commands if the test is True.

The picture on the right shows what the code looks like in the Python window. The Python IDE uses a range of colours for different types of word and symbol. The word `if` is a Python **key word**. Key words are used to build program structures in Python.

```
number1 = 70
number2 = 80
answer = input("do you want to add? (Y/N) ")
if answer == "Y":
    result = number1 + number2
    print(result)
```

In the Python IDE, key words are displayed in gold (dark yellow) font.

 **Activity**

Make a Python program by putting together all the commands shown above.

If and else in Scratch

In Scratch, the 'if… else' block has two spaces in it.

▶ The commands in the top space are carried out if the test is True.

▶ The commands in the lower space are carried out if the test is False.

The picture on the right shows an example of a Scratch program that uses 'if… else'.

If the test is True, the two numbers are added together. If the test is False, 'number2' is subtracted from 'number1'.

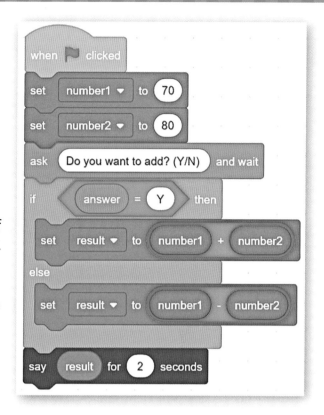

If and else in Python

To do the same thing in Python you enter the word `else` followed by a colon.

```
if answer == "Y":
    result = number1 + number2
else:
    result = number1 - number2
print(result)
```

Notice which commands are indented. These are the commands inside the conditional structure.

Activity

Make the Scratch program that uses the 'if… else' block.

Make the Python program that uses `if... else`.

Extra challenge

In the example in this lesson, the values of the variables 'number1' and 'number2' are set by the program.

▶ Make a version of the Scratch program where the user inputs the values of the two numbers.

▶ Make a Python program that does the same thing.

✔ Test

1 Here are some logical tests using Python relational operators. Which are True and which are False?

   a `4 == 5 - 1`

   b `55 >= 11 * 5`

   c `22 != 23 - 1`

2 Here is a Python program.

```
choice = input("enter X to exit the program")
if choice == "X":
    print("remember to log off")
else:
    print("you can make another menu choice")
```

   a The user entered the letter 'X'. What is the output of the program?

   b What other output can there be from this program? When will you see this output?

In this lesson

You will learn:

▶ how to increase the value of a variable

▶ how to use counter loops in Python and Scratch.

Spiral back

In previous books you made programs in Scratch that used a loop. Actions inside a loop are repeated. In this lesson you will discover how to use loop structure in Python programs.

Loops

Most programming languages allow you to put program commands inside a loop. Commands inside a loop are carried out many times. In Scratch there is a 'forever' loop. Commands inside the 'forever' loop will repeat until the program stops.

Most programming languages do not use 'forever' loops. In most programming languages, every loop has an **exit condition**. The exit condition is how you stop the loop. There are two types of loop. They have different exit conditions.

▶ A **counter loop** (or **fixed loop**) repeats a set number of times then stops.

▶ A **conditional loop** (or **condition-controlled loop**) is controlled by a logical test.

In this lesson you will make a program with a counter loop.

Scratch program with counter loop

Scratch Program 1 is a simple calculator. It asks the user to input two numbers. The program outputs the result of adding them together.

1

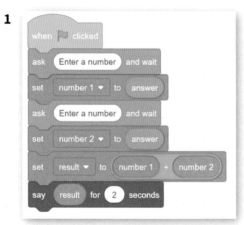

2

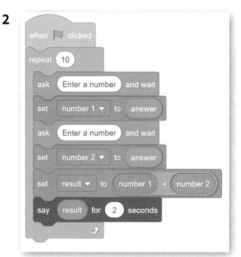

Scratch Program 2 is the same program. But in this version, all the commands are inside a counter loop. The number at the top of the loop tells you how many times the commands will be repeated.

When you run this program, the calculation will repeat 10 times. If you change the number, you change the number of repeats.

Python program with counter loop

In Python a counter loop is called a **for loop**. To make a loop that repeats 10 times the command is:

```
for i in range (10):
```

To make a loop that repeats 20 times the command is:

```
for i in range (20):
```

The lower-case letter `i` is the counter. You don't have to use the letter 'i' – you can use any name. But it is common for programmers to use the letter 'i'. The number in brackets sets the number of times the loop will repeat.

Python Program 1 adds two numbers together.

1
```
number1 = input("enter a number ")
number1 = int(number1)

number2 = input("enter a number ")
number2 = int(number2)

result = number1 + number2

print(result)
```

2
```
for i in range (10):
    number1 = input("enter a number ")
    number1 = int(number1)

    number2 = input("enter a number ")
    number2 = int(number2)

    result = number1 + number2
    print(result)
```

Python Program 2 is the same program with a counter loop.

The commands inside the loop are indented. The indented commands will repeat.

⚙️ Activity

Make the Scratch program and the Python program shown above. In each program, use a counter loop to repeat the commands.

Increase the value of a variable

In the programs you have just made, the user enters two numbers with each repeat of the loop. Each time, the program outputs the result of adding those two numbers.

But quite often in programming you will want to add to the previous total each time the commands repeat. To do this you need to create a new variable called 'total'.

Scratch program A sets 'total' to 0. Then it increases the value of 'total' by 1.

Scratch program B sets 'total' to 0. Then it increases the value of 'total' by adding a number that the user inputs.

A
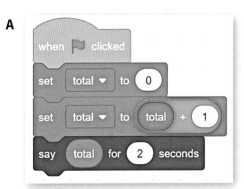

B
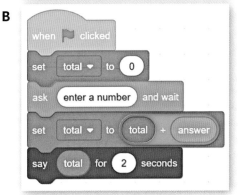

Plan to add up a total

You can use the command `total = total + number` to make a program that adds together 10 numbers.

Here is a plan for that program:

> Set the total to 0 at the start of the program.
>
> Loop 10 times:
>
>> Input a value.
>>
>> Add the input value to the total.
>
> Output the total at the end of the program.

Add up a total in Scratch

Look at the program plan in the table. For each line of the program you should know the matching Scratch command.

Planned action	Scratch block to use
Set total to 0	
Loop 10 times	
Input a value	
Add the input value to the total	
Output the total	

Activities

You can do either or both of these activities.

1 Copy and complete the table shown above. Note the Scratch block you would use to match each action.

2 Make a Scratch program to match the plan.

Increase a variable in Python

You have used the Scratch command to increase a variable. You can do the same thing in Python. This Python program sets `total` to 0. Then it increases the value of `total` by 1.

```
total = 0
total = total + 1
print(total)
```

This Python program sets 'total' to 0. Then it increase the value of 'total' by adding a number that the user inputs.

```
total = 0
number = input("enter a number ")
number = int(number)
total = total + number
print(total)
```

Remember in Python you need to convert user input to a number value before you do a calculation. That is the purpose of this command.

```
number = int(number)
```

Python program to add up a total

In Scratch you put the adding commands inside a loop. You can use Python to make the same program that you made in Scratch. You already know the Python commands that match each line of the plan.

Planned action	Python command
Set total to 0	`total = 0`
Loop 10 times	`for i in range (10):`
Input a value	`number = input("enter a number ")` `number = int(number)`
Add the input value to the total	`total = total + number`
Output the total	`print(total)`

If you fit these commands together, you will make a working program. Remember that Python will indent the commands inside the loop.

 **Activity**

Make a Python program to match the plan shown above. The program will use a counter loop. It will add 10 numbers to make a total.

In the last lesson you learned that `if` is a Python key word. The colour of key words in Python programs is gold. What other key words have you used in this program?

 Extra challenge

This Scratch program sets the variable 'total' to 100. Then it uses a counter loop to subtract 10 values from 'total'.

Make a Python program that does the same thing.

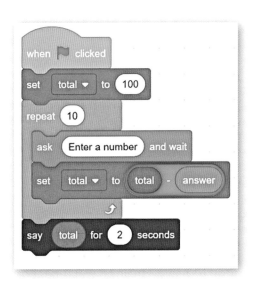

 Test

1 What does 'exit condition' mean?
2 What are the two types of loop?
3 Write the first line of a Python loop that repeats 100 times.
4 A Python program includes a variable called `points`. Write the command to increase `points` by 10.

In this lesson

You will learn:

▶ how to use a conditional loop in Scratch and Python.

What is a conditional loop?

In the last lesson you learned how to use a counter loop. Another name for a counter loop is a fixed loop, because the commands inside the fixed loop repeat a fixed number of times. You set the number of repeats at the top of the loop.

A conditional loop is different. It is controlled by a logical test. Every time the loop repeats, the computer tries the logical test again. The result of the logical test tells the computer whether to repeat the loop or stop.

Conditional loop in Scratch

This Scratch block makes a conditional loop.

The loop starts with the words 'repeat until'. Then there is a diamond-shaped space. A logical test block will fit into this space. The logical test will control the loop.

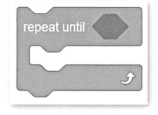

The loop will **repeat until** the test is True. Here is an example. Any commands that you insert inside the loop will repeat until the user enters '0'.

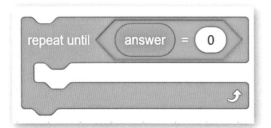

Adding up with a conditional loop

On the right is the finished Scratch program. It adds each new number that the user enters to the total. The loop will repeat until the user enters the value '0'.

The logical test in this program is:

'answer = 0'

The computer will check the logical test every time the loop repeats. The loop will repeat *until* the condition is True:

▶ If the condition is FALSE, the loop will CONTINUE.

▶ If the condition is TRUE, the loop will STOP.

When to use a conditional loop

Use a loop when you want to repeat commands inside a program.

▶ If you know exactly how many times you want to repeat the commands, use a counter loop.

▶ If you don't know exactly how many times you want to repeat the commands, use a conditional loop.

 **Activity**

Make a Scratch program to add each number that the user inputs to the total. Use a conditional loop. You can choose your own logical test for the conditional loop. Save and run the program. Correct any errors.

Conditional loop in Python

In Python a conditional loop is called a **while loop**. The first line of a while loop has these features:

▶ the word `while`

▶ a logical test

▶ a colon.

The computer will check the logical test every time the loop repeats. The loop will repeat *while* the condition is True:

▶ If the condition is TRUE, the loop will CONTINUE.

▶ If the condition is FALSE, the loop will STOP.

This is the other way round from Scratch.

What logical test?

You have to choose the logical test carefully.

In Scratch the loop stops when the test is True. The example program used this test:

'answer = 0'

In Python the loop stops when the test is False. You will use this test:

```
answer != 0
```

Remember: != means 'does not equal'.

▶ If the answer does not equal 0, the test is True. The loop will continue.

▶ If the answer equals 0, the test is False. The loop will stop.

The complete Python command to begin the conditional loop is:

```
while answer != 0:
```

Sully's program goes wrong

Sully made a Python program to add up a total. He used a conditional loop.
Here is Sully's program:

```
total = 0
while number != 0:
    number = input("enter a number ")
    number = int(number)
    total = total + number
print(total)
```

Sully's program did not work properly. Sully saw this error message:

```
  File "C:\temp.py", line 2
    while number != 0:
NameError: name 'number' is not defined
```

What has caused the problem? The error message told Sully the mistake is in
line 2:

```
  while number != 0:
```

The error message says: `name 'number' is not defined`.

The computer does not know what `number` means. This variable has not been
given a value yet. In Python, the computer cannot use a variable unless you have
given it a value. That means the computer cannot do the logical test.

Sully's program is still not right!

Sully decided to change the program. He found the command that assigns a value
to the variable `number` and the command that makes the variable into an integer.

```
  number = input("enter a number ")

  number = int(number)
```

He moved these commands to before the loop. Here is the new program:

```
total = 0
number = input("enter a number ")
number = int(number)
while number != 0:
    total = total + number
print(total)
```

When Sully ran the program, it started and asked him to enter a number. He
entered one value. But then the program stopped working. Nothing appeared on
the screen. Eventually Sully tried to close the Python Shell. He saw the message
shown on the right.

The message says the program is still running! Sully clicked OK to
'kill' the program. ('Kill' means stop the program running.) But what
went wrong?

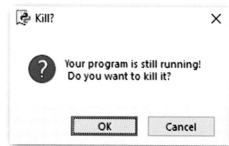

In this program there is no input inside the loop. The user cannot
enter a new number value. So there is no way to stop the loop.
The loop continues forever (until Sully closes the program).

Sully got it right

In the end, Sully changed the program again. He put input commands before the loop *and* inside the loop. This time, the program worked as planned. Here is Sully's new program:

```python
total = 0
number = input("enter a number ")
number = int(number)
while number != 0:
    total = total + number
    number = input("enter a number ")
    number = int(number)
print(total)
```

What Sully learned

To make a Python program with a conditional loop you have to do three things:

1 Start the loop with a logical test.

2 Assign a starting value to the test variable before the loop begins.

3 Give the user a chance to change the test variable inside the loop.

Because Sully did all three things, his program worked fine.

 Activity

Make the Python program shown in this lesson. Save and run the program. Correct any errors.

Extra challenge

▶ Make a Python program that adds each number that the user enters to the total until the user enters a value smaller than 0.

▶ Make a Python program that sets the variable `total` to 100 and subtracts numbers until the user enters a value greater than 99.

Test

1 In your own words, explain when to use a conditional loop in your program.

2 Here is a line from a Python program. What value of the variable `username` will cause the loop to stop?

```python
while username != "x":
```

3 Here is a Python program. It has an error in it. Explain what the error is.

```python
print("Start program")

while username != "x":

    username = input("enter your name ")

    print("hello", username)
```

4 Write the program without the error.

4.4 A class project

In this lesson

You will learn:

▶ how to apply Python skills to solve a problem

▶ how to spot syntax errors and fix them.

Counting up

Mr Shakir is a science teacher. His students are doing a biology project about bird populations. They have to count how many birds visit the school bird feeder. Mr Shakir has asked his students to write a Python program to count the number of bird visitors.

Here is the program requirement:

The user will input a 'Y' every time they see a bird at the table. When the program is finished it will output the total number of birds that visited the table.

The program will be called Bird Counter.

Class discussion

The class discussed what they needed to include in the Bird Counter program. Here are some of the students' ideas from their discussion:

▶ "We need a variable to store the number of birds."

▶ "Yes, and that number must start at 0."

▶ "We must have a loop, of course."

▶ "The loop must be a conditional loop because we don't know in advance how many birds we will see."

▶ "If it is a conditional loop, we have to think about the logical test. How do we stop the loop?"

Mr Shakir agreed with the students' ideas. He said, "Your ideas will help us make the program."

 **Activity**

Before you read any more of this lesson, try to make the Bird Counter program. Use the clues in the class discussion and the commands you learned in Lessons 4.1, 4.2 and 4.3 to help you make the program.

Program problems

Each student in Mr Shakir's class tried to write the Bird Counter program. But the students made some errors.

All programmers make errors when they write programs. A good programmer can recognise errors and fix them. Then their programs work the way they planned. The Python IDE has features to help you find and fix errors:

▶ colour and layout when you write the program

▶ error messages when you run the program.

In this lesson you will learn to recognise and fix common program errors in Python.

Syntax errors

Every programming language has rules. The rules of a language are called **syntax**. If you break the rules of a programming language, you make a **syntax error**.

In Unit 3 you learned what happens when you run a program:

1 **Translating**: The computer turns the commands into machine code.

2 **Running**: The computer executes the machine code commands.

If there is a syntax error, the computer cannot understand the commands. It cannot translate them into machine code. The computer will stop. It will show you an error message.

Fixing the problems

Mr Shakir checked the programs his students made.

He wrote this note for his students. It lists the most common syntax errors that he found.

> *Most common syntax errors*
> *Using the wrong word*
> *Not using indent*
> *Leaving out the : sign*
> *Single = instead of double ==*

Using the wrong word

Abdel is one of Mr Shakir's students. He mixed up Scratch and Python.

In Scratch a conditional loop begins 'repeat until'.

In Python a conditional loop begins `while`.

Abdel typed 'repeat until' in a Python program. Here is the error message he saw.

The message says there is a syntax error. It has highlighted the line where the error is. This helped Abdel to fix the problem.

Python makes it easy to spot where the error is. It marks the error with a red block.

```
total = 0
visitor = input("type Y if you see a bird ")
repeat until visitor == "Y":
    visitor = input("type Y if you see a bird ")
    total = total + 1
print(total)
```

SyntaxError ✕

❌ invalid syntax

OK

Not using indent

In Python, commands inside a loop are indented. Python adds the indentation automatically. But Stefan made a mistake – he removed the indentation.

Here is the error message he saw:

The error message says 'expected an indented block'. That helped Stefan to understand what was wrong with his program.

```
total = 0
visitor = input("type Y if you see
while visitor == "Y":
visitor = input("
total = total + 1
print(total)
```

SyntaxError ✕

✕ expected an indented block

OK

Leaving out the colon

Lots of Python commands end with a colon (two dots). Here are some examples.

```
if answer == 12:

for i in range (15):

while answer > 9:
```

If you leave out the colon the program will go wrong. Kamal made this mistake. Here is the error message that he saw. The red block shows where the error is. Kamal could see what was wrong and fix the problem.

```
total = 0
visitor = input("type Y if you see a b
while visitor == "Y"
    visitor = input("type
    total = total + 1
print(total)
```

SyntaxError ✕

✕ invalid syntax

OK

Using a single equals sign

The equals sign is used in Python for two different things:

▶ To assign a value to a variable use a single equals sign =.

▶ To make a logical test use a double equals sign ==.

Milan decided to make a variable called `visitor`. The user of the program will type 'Y' every time they see a bird visitor to the bird feeder.

The next command includes a logical test. It tests whether the variable `visitor` holds the value 'Y'.

```
while visitor == "Y"
```

Milan forgot to use the double equals sign in his logical test. This is the error message he saw.

Milan wasn't sure what had gone wrong. He had used the equals sign in other parts of the program. Why was that equals sign wrong, but all the others were correct? Mr Shakir reminded Milan about how to use the equals sign in Python. Then Milan was able to fix the error.

```
total = 0
visitor = input("type Y if you see a
while visitor = "Y":
    visitor = input("t
    total = total + 1
print(total)
```

SyntaxError ✕

✕ invalid syntax

OK

 **Activities**

1   Here is a plan for the completed Bird Counter program. Copy and complete the table. Fill in the correct Python code for every line of the plan. Watch out for syntax errors.

Plan	Python code
Set the total to 0	
Input the variable `visitor`	
Loop while `visitor` holds the value 'Y'	
Add one to the total	
Input the variable `visitor` again	
Print out the total	

2   If you have not done it already, make the Bird Counter program in Python. The program will count the number of bird visitors to a bird feeder.

3   Write a note to users of the Bird Counter program. You can use a word processor or write the note by hand. Your note must explain:

   a   what the program does

   b   what to type if you see a bird visitor to the bird feeder

   c   what to type when you want to stop recording bird visitors and see the result.

Extra challenge

In Activity 3, you wrote a note to users of your program. Now change your program so it will display this information on the screen. Add print commands to do this.

Why is showing this information within the program better than putting it in a separate note?

Be creative

Make a resource to teach students about syntax errors. You could create a poster, a presentation or even a video.

 Test

1   Syntax errors stop the computer from translating the program. What does 'translating the program' mean?

2   Name one place in a Python program where you must include a colon.

3   Text colour can help you find errors in your Python programs. Give one example.

4   In your own words, explain the difference between a single equals sign and a double equals sign in Python.

In this lesson

You will learn:

▶ how to spot logical errors in a program

▶ how to check that a program works as you intended.

Logical errors

In the last lesson you learned about syntax errors. If a program has syntax errors the computer cannot translate the program into machine code. The program will not run. The computer will show you an error message.

In this lesson you will learn about **logical errors**. A logical error means that the logic of the program is wrong. The program works but it does the wrong thing. It does not meet the requirement.

It can be hard to spot a logical error because:

▶ You can run the program.

▶ The computer executes all the commands.

▶ You don't see an error message.

A new purpose

In the last lesson, some students made a Bird Counter program to count the number of birds visiting a bird feeder. The program works like this:

▶ If a bird visits the bird feeder, type the letter 'Y'.

▶ The count goes up by one.

Mr Shakir's students shared the Bird Counter program with students in another school called North Mountain School. This school is in a colder country. In that country lots of birds visit the school bird feeder, especially during the winter.

The students at North Mountain School found it difficult to use the Bird Counter program made by Mr Shakir's students. The Bird Counter program records bird visitors one at a time. But at North Mountain School the birds arrive at the feeder in groups. The students decided to make a new program.

Discuss and plan

The students discussed how they wanted the new program to work. They wrote the requirement for their program:

The students decided to call their program the Bird Addition program.

> ## Program requirement
> ▶ Each student will watch the bird feeder for one minute.
> ▶ They will count how many birds visit the feeder in one minute.
> ▶ They will enter that value as a number.
> ▶ When all the students have entered a value, the program will output the total.

 **Activity**

Before you go any further, try to make the Bird Addition program to meet the program requirement.

Input a number

In the old Bird Counter program, the user enters the value 'Y' if they see a bird. In the new Bird Addition program, the user enters a number.

The students at North Mountain School made several changes to the program:

▶ Instead of having a variable called `visitor`, the variable is now called `visits`. The `visits` variable will store the number of visits to the bird feeder.

▶ The user prompt is different – it reminds the user to enter a number.

▶ The input that the user enters must be changed to integer data type so it can be used in calculations.

Here is the program with these changes made. The program does not work yet.

This program has several problems. Can you see the problems? If you are not sure, enter this code in a Python file and run the program. Does the program run? Does the program meet the requirement?

```
total = 0
visits = input("enter the number of visits")
visits = int(visits)
while visits == "Y":
    visits = input("enter number of visits")
    visits = int(visits)
    total = total + 1
print(total)
```

Exit condition

The program has a while loop. The logical test is:

```
visits == "Y"
```

This does not work. In the new program, the variable `visits` stores a number not a letter so the logical test is never True. The commands inside the loop never happen.

The students decided to change the exit condition. The loop will continue if the number of visits is anything but 0. If the user enters the number 0 the loop will stop. The new test is:

```
visits != 0
```

The students ran the Bird Addition program. The program started and the commands inside the loop were repeated. But when the students used the program to record visits to their bird feeder, they found a problem. Sometimes no birds visited the bird feeder. The user had to input the number 0. But when they entered 0 the program stopped.

```
total = 0
visits = input("enter the number of visits")
visits = int(visits)
while visits != 0:
    visits = input("enter number of visits")
    visits = int(visits)
    total = total + 1
print(total)
```

That is because when the value of `visits` is 0 the test is False, so the loop stops. In the next activity you will find out how to solve this problem.

Change the exit condition

The students need to change the logical test:

▶ The logical test has to be a number comparison.

▶ The number has to be one that will never be a real number of birds.

For example, the students could choose a negative number. Instead, they chose the number 99. If the user types '99' the loop will stop. The students know there will never be 99 birds at the feeder.

But the Bird Addition program is still not ready. Can you see why?

```
total = 0
visits = input("enter the number of visits")
visits = int(visits)
while visits != 99:
    visits = input("enter number of visits")
    visits = int(visits)
    total = total + 1
print(total)
```

Add up the visitors

The program has to add up the total number of birds. At the moment the program adds just one to the total every time the user enters a number.

The students changed the Bird Addition program so that it adds the number of visitors to the total.

```
total = 0
visits = input("enter the number of visits")
visits = int(visits)
while visits != 99:
    visits = input("enter number of visits")
    visits = int(visits)
    total = total + visits
print(total)
```

But this program is still wrong! Can you see why? If you are not sure, enter this code in a Python file, then run the program. What goes wrong?

Change the order of commands

There are two problems:

▶ The first input value is NOT added to the total (the one that is input before the loop starts).

▶ The final input value IS added to the total (the value 99).

To avoid these problems the students reversed the order of commands inside the loop:

First add the input number to the total.

Then enter a new number.

When the user enters the exit value (99), the program stops right away. Here is the program with that change made.

This program works! The students have found and fixed all the logical errors.

```
total = 0
visits = input("enter the number of visits")
visits = int(visits)
while visits != 99:
    total = total + visits
    visits = input("enter number of visits")
    visits = int(visits)
print(total)
```

 **Activity**

If you have not done it already, make the Bird Addition program. It should add up the total number of birds that visit a bird feeder.

 **Extra challenge**

Some students chose to make a different program, with a counter loop. There were 20 students in the class so they used a counter loop that counted up to 20. Write a Python program that does this.

 Test

1. Why is it harder for a programmer to spot a logical error than a syntax error?
2. Look at the addition program you made. What would happen if the line `total = 0` were included inside the loop?
3. Write a Python program that adds together five numbers input by the user.

Digital citizen of the future

Errors that stop programs working properly are called 'bugs'. Software companies test their programs for bugs before they offer them for sale. If a program is used for fun – for example, a game – a few bugs in the code don't matter so much.

But some software programs are very important – for example: software in a hospital that measures a patient's heart rate; software in a factory that controls a dangerous chemical reaction; software in a bank that looks after the customers' money. These programs must not include any mistakes.

One day you may be a programmer who writes important software. Or you may work in a hospital, factory or bank and use important software. You will need to make sure that the software program has been thoroughly tested so that the software is reliable.

In this lesson

You will learn:

▶ how to make your programs user friendly

▶ how to make your programs readable.

Make user-friendly programs

Users like programs that are **user friendly**. That means the programs are easy to use. Some things that make a program easy to use are:

▶ simple inputs with prompts

▶ clear outputs

▶ other messages to explain the program.

The program commands that handle inputs and outputs are called the **interface**. The user enters inputs through the interface. The user sees the outputs displayed in the interface.

When you program in Scratch it is it easy to make a user-friendly interface. On the right is an example.

> Type the number of birds you saw

The Scratch interface includes colourful backdrops and sprites. But Python only has plain text. The interface is not so user friendly. In this lesson you will learn to make a Python program with a more user-friendly interface.

The interface of your program

You made a program to count visitors to a bird feeder. This is what the user sees when they use the program.

This program is not very user friendly. It is not clear what inputs are needed or what the output means. Now you will improve the program.

```
enter number of visits2
enter number of visits5
enter number of visits9
enter number of visits99
16
```

Simple inputs and prompts

You need to make it easy for your user to enter the right inputs. Here are some tips:

▶ Make the input short and simple to enter. For example, ask the user to input 'Y' instead of 'Yes'. This is less work for the user. There is less chance of an error.

▶ Add a prompt. The prompt is the text inside the brackets. It tells the user exactly what they should enter. This means the user feels less stressed. It will help the user to avoid making an error.

▶ If you include a space at the end of the prompt, the interface looks better. There is a space between the prompt and what the user enters.

Here is a bad input command:

```
continue = input("continue?")
```

Here is a better version:

```
continue = input("do you want to continue? (Y/N) ")
```

Which makes it clearer what you have to do?

Clear outputs

Most programs end with an output. It might be a number, such as the total number of birds seen. To make your programs user friendly, add some text to the print command. That helps the user to know what the output is.

Here is a bad output command:

```
print(total)
```

Here is a better version:

```
print("we saw this many birds", total)
```

The explanation and the variable are separated by commas.

Other on-screen messages

Use the `print` command to add messages to your program. For example, you can add a title and explain what the program does.

The students changed their program to make the interface more user friendly.

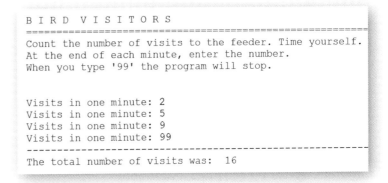

```
B I R D   V I S I T O R S
==========================================================
Count the number of visits to the feeder. Time yourself.
At the end of each minute, enter the number.
When you type '99' the program will stop.


Visits in one minute: 2
Visits in one minute: 5
Visits in one minute: 9
Visits in one minute: 99
----------------------------------------------------------
The total number of visits was:   16
```

Other useful print commands

Here are some other print commands that are useful for this activity.

Include `"\n"` in a print command to make a new line:

```
print("\n")
```

Use the 'multiplication' operator to repeat a symbol. This command will print ten dashes:

```
print("-" * 10)
```

 **Activity**

Open the Bird Addition program. Add extra features to make it more user friendly.

 **Explore more**

Talk to family and friends about what apps and programs they find easiest to use. What makes a program 'user friendly'? You might find that different people want different types of software. If you have time, write a report on what you have found.

Make readable programs

Programmers like programs that are **readable**. That means the program itself is easy to read and understand. Often, more than one programmer works on the same program. Making readable programs is good for teamwork.

Making your programs readable will help you to be a better programmer. When you come back to your work, you will find it easy to remember what you did. You will find it easy to improve and change your program. Creating readable programs helps everyone.

Two things that make a program easy to read are:

▶ well-chosen variable names   ▶ comments.

Variable names

You have learned how to make good variable names. The name of a variable should tell you what value the variable stores. When other programmers look at your program they will understand your work.

This code is not readable because we don't know what the variable x stores:

```
x = input("value")
```

This code is much more readable because it is clear what the variable cost stores:

```
cost = input("enter the item cost ")
```

Comments

Comments are messages you add to your program. In Python you mark a comment with the hash symbol #.

Any text that you enter after the # symbol is not part of the program. The computer will see the # symbol in your code. It will ignore the rest of the line. But other programmers will be able to read the comment. You can use comments to add explanations and other messages about your program. That will make the program more readable.

Some students decided to make the Bird Addition program more readable. This is what the program looked like.

```
# This program records total visits to a bird feeder
total = 0

# display the user interface
print("B I R D  V I S I T O R S")
print("=" * 60)
print("Count the number of visits to the feeder. Time yourself.")
print("At the end of each minute, enter the number.")
print("When you type '99' the program will stop.")
print("\n")

# input number of visits
visits = input("Visits in one minute: ")
visits = int(visits)

# repeat until '99' entered
while visits != 99:
    total = total + visits
    visits = input("Visits in one minute: ")
    visits = int(visits)

# output the result
print("-" * 60)
print("The total number of visits was: ",total)
```

 **Activity**

Add features to improve the readability of your program.

Take the program to a new level

Mrs Li is a new biology teacher at North Mountain School. She is very keen on studying birds. She wants to use the program the students had made. But she asks for an extra feature:

▶ "Can the program tell me the average number of birds that arrive in one minute?"

The students adapt their program to meet Mrs Li's requirement.

Calculate an average

The program has to calculate the average of a series of numbers. To calculate an average you need to know two things:

▶ the total of all the numbers added together

▶ the count of how many numbers there were in the series.

The average is the total divided by the count.

Discuss and plan

The students were confident they could do this task. They had a discussion to plan the program. Here are some things they said.

▶ "We need a new variable called count or counter that starts at 0."

▶ "This variable will go up by one every time the user enters a number."

▶ "At the end, we can use this variable to calculate the average."

 Extra challenge

1 Adapt the program to calculate the average number of bird visitors. Use the students' comments to help you make these changes.

2 Make sure the program is readable and usable.

✓ **Test**

1 Say one way that Scratch is more user friendly than Python.

2 Hayley wrote a command to print a variable. How can she change the print command to make it more user friendly?

3 Why do well-chosen variable names make your programs more readable?

4 Explain how adding comments to a program might help you next time you work on the program.

Check what you know

You have learned

▶ how to use conditional (if) structures in Python

▶ how to make Python programs with loops

▶ how to find and fix errors in programs

▶ how make your programs user friendly and readable.

Try the test and activities. They will help you to see how much you understand.

Test

Kumar wrote a program to find the largest of two numbers.

When he ran the program, he saw this error message:

```
number1 = input()
number1 = int(number1)
number2 = input()
number2 = int(number2)
if number1 > number2
    largest = number1
else:
    largest = number2
print(largest)
```

SyntaxError	×
✕ invalid syntax	
	OK

1 The message says 'SyntaxError'. What is syntax?

2 Line 5 has a syntax error. Rewrite this line without the error.

Poppy wrote a program to add together all the items in a bill to give a total.

```
total = 0

while variable > 0:
    total = total + variable
    variable = input()
    variable = int(variable)

print(total)
```

3 An error in this program will prevent it from running. What is the error?

4 Rewrite the program without this error.

5 Describe one way you could make this program more user friendly.

6 Describe one way you could make this program more readable.

A student made a program to check passcodes. The program asks you to input your passcode and tells you whether it is correct or wrong.

```
enter your passcode: 88089
login successful
```

The correct passcode is the string '88089'.

Program 1

Do as much as you can of this activity.

▶ Make a Python program which asks the user to enter the passcode.

▶ Extend the program with an `if` structure:

- If the user enters the correct passcode, the program outputs the message `"login successful"`.

- Else, it outputs the message `"login failed"`.

Program 2

Attempt this activity if you have finished Program 1. Do as much as you can in the time available.

▶ Replace the conditional structure with a `while` loop. The loop will repeat while the passcode is wrong. Inside the loop the program asks the user to input the passcode again.

▶ If you have time, extend the program so that it records the number of attempts needed to enter the correct passcode. It then outputs the number of attempts.

▶ Make the program as user friendly and readable as you can.

Self-evaluation

- I answered test questions 1 and 2.

- I began to make Program 1.

- I answered test questions 1–4.

- I completed Program 1 and it worked.

- I answered all the test questions.

- I completed at least part of Program 2 and it worked.

Re-read any parts of the unit you feel unsure about. Try the test and activities again – can you do more this time?

5 Multimedia: Make a podcast

You will learn

▶ how to plan a podcast by creating an outline and script

▶ how to record digital audio using your computer

▶ how to edit and improve digital audio recordings using digital audio workstation (DAW) software

▶ how to use feedback to improve your podcast.

A **podcast** is a sound recording similar to a radio programme. A podcast is shared over the world wide web. Podcasts are usually made as a series of episodes. They can be published daily, weekly or monthly.

You can download a podcast file to your device or **stream** it from a podcast hosting service.

Anyone can record and share podcasts – you just need access to recording equipment and the internet.

In this unit, you will plan and record a podcast. You will use digital recording hardware and software to make your podcast.

Podcasting across the world

The number of people who listen to podcasts is increasing very quickly. Podcasts are particularly popular in Asia. A survey showed that 58% of people in South Korea listened to at least one podcast episode in one month in 2018.

Many radio stations now make their programmes available as podcasts. Podcast listeners are often younger than traditional radio audiences. This means that the number of podcasts and listeners will probably keep growing in the future.

 **Unplugged**

In this unit, you will make a pilot episode for a podcast. Media companies make pilot episodes so they can test an idea with their audience.

Discuss ideas for a podcast episode that you can make individually. For example:

▶ **things that you do in school** – your favourite lessons, school trips or school club activities

▶ **things that you do at home** – your hobbies, holidays or sports activities.

Choose one idea for your own podcast pilot episode. Write the idea down.

Talk about…

Podcasts often have similar content to radio programmes, but you listen to them in a different way. Compare podcasts and traditional radio programmes. Talk about the advantages and disadvantages of each. Which is best for the way you live?

Did you know?

A recent estimate suggests that there are over 750,000 podcasts in the world. Together, they have 30 million episodes. That's a lot of listening!

> podcast
> track clip multi-track
> mono trim looped playback
> parameters mix safety copy
> stream script

5.1 Plan a podcast

In this lesson

You will learn:

▶ how to plan a podcast

▶ how to write a podcast outline and script.

Spiral back

 In Student Book 6 you learned how to add audio recordings to your presentations. In this unit, you will build on your skills to plan, make and share an episode of a podcast.

Making and sharing a podcast

Podcasters use an application (app) called an audio editor or digital audio workstation (DAW) to make recordings. Like a broadcast radio programme, a podcast can have speech and music. Using audio editing software allows you to record the speech and music separately and then edit and combine them to create your podcast. Podcasts are shared using a hosting service that specialises in streaming audio.

How to plan your podcast

You have already thought of some ideas for a podcast. Now you need to turn your ideas into a plan. There are three things you can think about to help you plan:

1 **Your aim:** This is the purpose of your podcast. Ask yourself: what do you want the listeners to know or understand after listening to your podcast? How do you want them to feel after they have heard your podcast?

2 **Your objectives:** What things do you need to tell your listeners in your podcast so that you achieve your aim?

3 **Your constraints:** How long do you want your podcast to be? (How many minutes?) Setting a time limit will help you focus on the content that is most important.

When you make a plan, constraints are very important because they are things that cannot be changed. Your aims and objectives often need to change so that you can achieve them despite your constraints.

Start by writing down your aim in creating your podcast. It should look similar to this:

Aim: I'm going to create a _____ minute podcast to tell my audience about _____ _____ _____.

Now that you have set an aim and a time limit, you can begin to think about your objectives for the content of your podcast.

Choose the content

Think about the best way to present content in your podcast. Here are some of the options for presenting content.

Presentation style

▶ Solo presentation – You present your content alone.

▶ Co-hosting – You present your content together with one or more others.

▶ Interview – You ask a guest questions to get their opinions or expert knowledge about a subject.

Location

▶ In the studio – You and your co-host or interviewees are indoors in a recording studio. You could even be in different studios if you are using Skype or a similar audio chat service to carry out your interview.

▶ On location – You record your content outside of the studio, using a portable device.

Mood

▶ Formal and informative – You use formal language and share detailed information with your audience. This style suits serious subjects.

▶ Informal and entertaining – You use less formal language and aim to make your audience feel good, smile or laugh.

Make an outline plan

Your podcast should have a structure. You need to carefully plan the order of the different parts of the podcast. In media production, the parts of a show are sometimes called segments.

You can use an outline to help you structure your podcast. An outline gives the order of the segments and briefly says what the different segments will include. Some common segments are:

▶ **Intro** – Explain who you are and what the podcast is about.

▶ **Jingle (or 'sting')** – A short piece of music will help people recognise and remember your podcast.

▶ **Topic segment** – Use one or more segments to cover the topic (subject) of your podcast. Each segment can have a different type of content, such as an interview or solo presentation.

▶ **Outro** – Give a short summary of the topic segments and a conclusion.

▶ **Closing remarks** – Thank the audience for listening. Encourage them to listen to the next episode.

Here is an example of a podcast outline.

Podcast title	The School Sports Podcast	Length		5 minutes
Segment	**Content**		**Timing**	
Intro	Greet the listeners. Say my name. Say that this podcast is about sports at school. Say that this episode will be an interview with the captain of the school ~~football~~ soccer team.		30–60 seconds	
Jingle	Play the School Sports jingle. Fade jingle out after 7 seconds!		10 seconds	
Topic 1: Interview	Introduce and welcome the soccer captain. Ask how successful the school team is.		3 minutes	

> The outline stage is a good time to think about the audience. For example, are they more likely to understand the word 'soccer' or 'football'?

Write a script

Most podcasts sound informal and natural. It takes a lot of practice to sound natural and relaxed while you are trying to remember everything in your outline plan. Most podcasters use a script for at least a part of their podcast.

Your script includes some or all of the exact words you want to say in a segment. When you write a script, remember to:

▶ **Write like you speak** – Use everyday words so you sound natural and relaxed.

▶ **Use short sentences** – This will make your content easier to understand.

▶ **Avoid jargon** (specialist words and abbreviations) – Your listeners might not know very much about your subject.

Script
Hi, my name is Melissa and I'm your host for this week's School Sports Podcast – where you can find out everything about the sports clubs in our school. This week we'll be talking about the school soccer team. I'll be asking the team captain, Saida, how you can join the team.

Music

In your outline plan, write down ideas about the type of music you want to include. Where do you want to use music in your podcast? What kind of mood are you trying to create? This will help you search for music clips later.

 **Activity**

 You can use the file 'My podcast outline' for this activity.

Review your podcast ideas from the Unplugged activity. Choose one idea for the pilot episode of your new podcast.

Use the outline template to complete your podcast outline:

▶ Write down the aim of your podcast and the length of the pilot episode – no more than 5 minutes.

▶ Complete the 'Content' column for each segment of your podcast, including the music.

▶ Add a 'Script' column to your outline. Write the script for each segment that you think needs some scripted content.

Save your work.

 **Extra challenge**

Podcasts often have a web page with notes for listeners, called 'show notes'. The show notes are often mentioned in the podcast so listeners know where to find them. Show notes can include text, images, graphics and links to other websites. What material do you think will be useful in show notes for your podcast's audience?

 Test

1. What do the letters 'DAW' stand for?
2. Put these stages of planning into the correct order: script, aim, outline.
3. Explain the difference between an outline and a script for a podcast.
4. Give an example of a constraint on your plans for a podcast.

In this lesson

You will learn:

▶ how computers record sound digitally

▶ how to make sound recordings using multi-track audio software.

How is sound captured digitally?

Sound is movement of the air. The air moves in a wave pattern called sound waves. Our ears can detect these sound waves. A microphone can also detect sound waves.

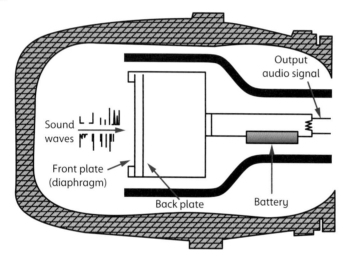

A microphone has a part that vibrates when sound waves hit it. In most microphones the part that vibrates is a diaphragm. The microphone also has an electromagnet that generates electricity when the diaphragm vibrates. A computer converts the electricity to a digital signal.

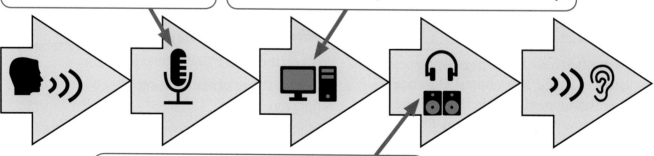

1 A microphone converts sound waves into electricity.

2 A computer converts the electrical current into digital data. It stores the data. It can play the sound by converting the data back into electricity.

3 Headphones or loudspeakers turn the electrical current back into sound waves you can hear.

Digital audio formats

The table lists some common audio file types and describes their features and uses.

File type	Filename extension	Features	Used for ...
WAV	.wav	Stores audio accurately and with high quality. WAV files can be very large so they can take a long time to copy and process. Not suitable for portable players or streaming.	high-quality recording of audio such as music and speech The WAV format is used in professional recording studios.
MP3	.mp3	Uses much less storage space than WAV. MP3 files are compressed, so there is some loss of audio quality. You can vary the amount of **compression** to make file sizes smaller.	storing and playing back audio on personal devices streaming audio over the internet Professionally recorded music is often converted to MP3 for distribution to listeners.
FLAC	.flac	Provides lossless compression – file sizes are reduced but there is no loss of quality.	storing and playing audio on personal devices such as laptops and PCs

In the example in this unit, sound is recorded as a WAV file. It can be converted to MP3 for streaming later.

How to use your computer to record sound

To begin recording sound, you need a microphone connected to your computer. Different microphones are appropriate in different circumstances.

Microphone	Features	Used for ...
External microphone (condenser type) 	High-quality audio capture. Very sensitive to background noise, so needs a quiet environment.	high-quality audio from voice or instruments
External microphone (headset) 	Medium-quality audio capture or professional-quality for broadcasting. Must be positioned close to the speaker's mouth, so it can only pick up sound from one person.	internet voice communications broadcasting such as sports commentary
Internal microphone (laptop, tablet, smartphone)	Medium-quality audio capture. Laptop microphones can capture sound from more than one person – but also pick up some background noise.	internet voice communications

Recording software

Many computers and smartphones have simple voice recorders that allow you to record a single piece of audio. These apps offer very few options to edit the sound. They can only record and play back one **track** of audio.

To create a podcast featuring more than one voice, you will need to record more than one track. Each track can contain pieces of audio called **clips**. You can arrange and mix the tracks together to create your final audio project. This process is called **multi-track** recording and editing. The software you use for this is often called a digital audio workstation (DAW).

Choosing a digital audio workstation (DAW)

Many audio-editing apps are free to download and use, such as Audacity, WavePad, Ocenaudio and Wavosaur for Windows or GarageBand for iOS.

The example in this unit uses the Audacity DAW. You can use any multi-track DAW that works on your device.

Using a DAW

Most DAWs have a screen that shows the sound in your project as waveforms. The waveforms are arranged into different tracks (from top to bottom) along a timeline (from left to right). A cursor moves from left to right as you play the sound. The cursor is usually shown as a line across all the tracks.

This is how the Audacity project screen looks.

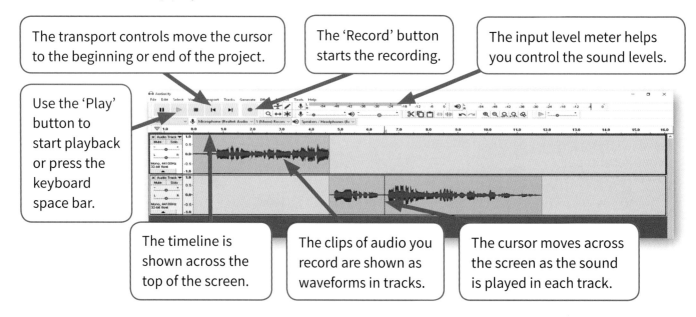

The transport controls move the cursor to the beginning or end of the project.

The 'Record' button starts the recording.

The input level meter helps you control the sound levels.

Use the 'Play' button to start playback or press the keyboard space bar.

The timeline is shown across the top of the screen.

The clips of audio you record are shown as waveforms in tracks.

The cursor moves across the screen as the sound is played in each track.

Set the recording levels

Make sure that your microphone and speakers or headphones are correctly set up.

1 Click in the area of the screen with the input level meter.

2 Speak into the microphone in your normal voice.

3 While you are speaking, move the recording volume slider until the green lines reach about two-thirds of the way across the meter.

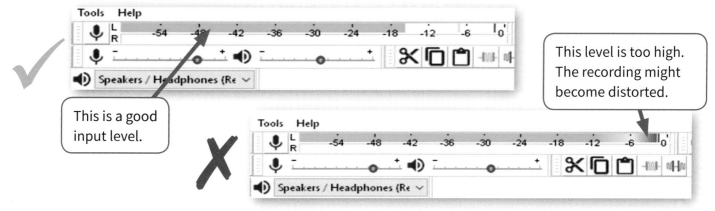

This is a good input level.

This level is too high. The recording might become distorted.

Making a recording

Click on the 'Record' button and begin speaking. The cursor will start to move from left to right and a waveform graphic will appear. The waveform shows the sound you are recording.

When you have finished recording, click 'Stop'. To listen to your track, move the cursor to the beginning of the project and click 'Play'.

 **Activity**

Make a test recording.

▶ Set up your microphone. Check the input level meter until you are happy with the level.

▶ Record one minute of test audio. Choose a segment of your podcast. Use the outline and the script you created in the last lesson.

▶ Stop the recording and listen to it.

▶ Write down any changes and improvements you would like to make in the final recording.

 **Extra challenge**

Record a second test segment.

▶ Add a new track from the 'Tracks' menu and place the cursor in the new track area, at the end of the timeline.

▶ Record your second test segment.

 Test

1 In your DAW, what does the waveform illustrate?

2 Write down this sentence and fill in the gaps: "A microphone converts _____ into _____."

3 How does an input level meter help you record audio?

4 Explain the difference between an audio track and an audio clip.

In this lesson

You will learn:

▶ how to record more than one track of audio

▶ how to check the quality of your recording

▶ how to edit the length of your recordings

▶ how to arrange your recordings along the timeline.

Set up and make your podcast

In the last lesson, you set up your recording equipment and created a test recording. Now it is time to record your podcast. Follow these steps:

▶ Set up your recording equipment in a quiet place with very little background noise.

▶ Decide how you will record the segments in your outline.
  • You can record each segment on a separate track.
  • If you are very confident, you can record all the segments on one track and separate them for editing later.

▶ Practise each segment before you record. You will feel more relaxed if you know your content.

▶ Press 'Record' and have fun making your podcast.

Record segments as separate tracks

Record each podcast segment on its own track. You can then edit the tracks and arrange them so that they flow together without gaps.

Start by recording your first segment as 'Track 1'. Follow the instructions for recording in the previous lesson. When you are ready to record the next segment, add a new track in your DAW software.

Adding more tracks to your recording

In Audacity, you can add a new track from the 'Tracks' menu.

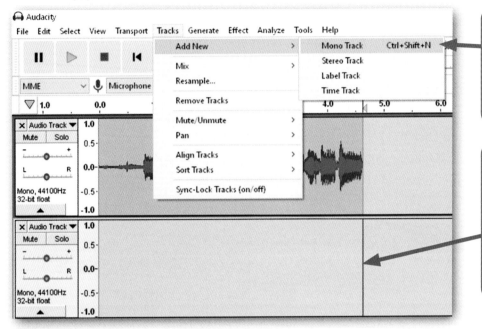

Add a new track. A **mono** track is suitable for a podcast voice recording. A mono track uses a single **channel** of audio.

Place the cursor in the new track area, after the end of the first segment. The recording on this track will start from this point. Make sure you have selected the correct track.

Trim tracks

When you make a recording, there is usually a pause between when you press 'Record' and when you start talking. There is usually a pause at the end of the track too, between when you stop talking and when you press 'Stop'.

You can **trim** your tracks. This means you delete any unwanted silence at the beginning and the end of the track.

To trim the beginning of your track, use the playback controls to play the track from the beginning. Click 'Pause' when the sound starts. Click on the waveform to position the cursor just before the sound starts.

You can do the same to trim the end of the track. Position the cursor at the correct place on the waveform, then open the 'Select' menu and choose 'Region', then 'Cursor to Track End'.

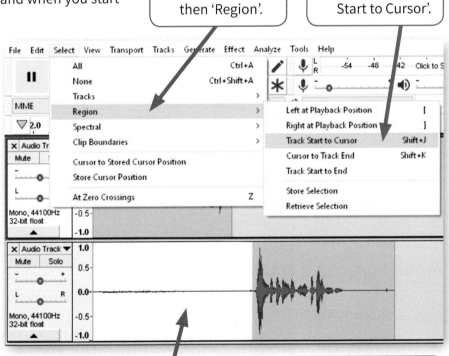

1 Choose 'Select', then 'Region'.

2 Choose 'Track Start to Cursor'.

3 The area before the cursor is now highlighted. Press the 'Delete' button on your keyboard to remove this area.

4 Now, when you play back your file, your voice will start straight away.

Edit audio in a track

Everyone makes mistakes when they are recording audio. You might misread a word or cough. It doesn't matter, because you can fix your mistakes by editing the track.

Use the playback controls to play your audio file and listen for parts you want to edit.

When you have found a part you want to remove, click the 'Pause' button.

> **1** Select the 'Zoom' tool and click to zoom in on an area of the track. Right-click to zoom back out.

> **2** Use the 'Selection' tool to place the cursor and highlight areas of the waveform.

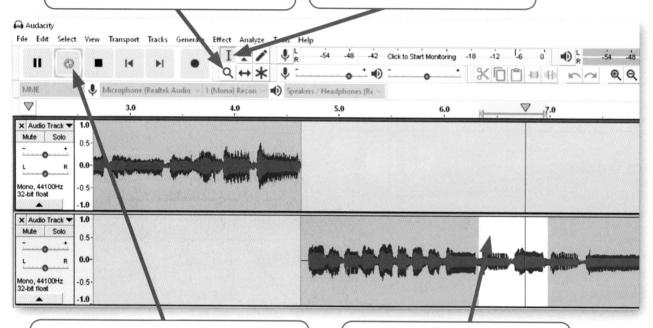

> **4** Use the **looped playback** function to check your selection is correct. Press 'Shift' on your keyboard and click the 'Play' button to start looped playback.

> **3** Select the area. Click and drag to highlight your selection. Drag the edge of the area to make it bigger or smaller.

To delete the selected area, press the 'Delete' key on your keyboard.

Move audio in a track

When you have edited audio in a track, you might find that the track no longer lines up with other tracks. Trimming the start of one track might mean that it starts before another track finishes. Trimming the end of one track might leave a gap before the audio on the next track starts.

You can move the audio in a track to make it line up again.

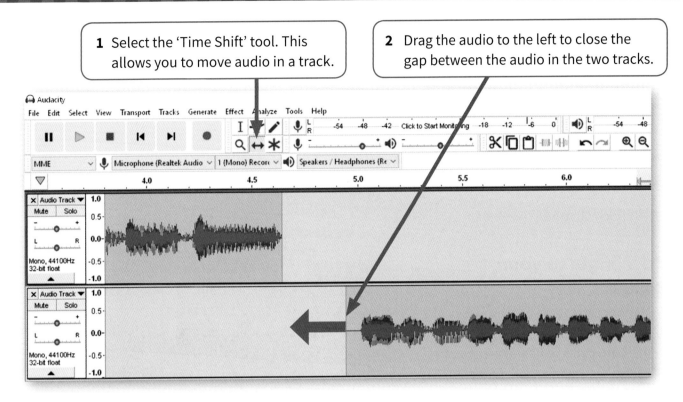

1 Select the 'Time Shift' tool. This allows you to move audio in a track.

2 Drag the audio to the left to close the gap between the audio in the two tracks.

Listen to the result when you have moved the audio. Sometimes a small gap between tracks sounds better than no gap.

 **Activity**

Record the segments of your podcast on separate tracks.

Play back your audio and decide what edits you need to make.

Use the trimming and time shift tools to edit your tracks.

Listen to the whole file to check you have a complete podcast programme.

Save your work.

 **Extra challenge**

Your DAW gives every audio track a default name. In Audacity, the name is 'Audio Track'. Name the different tracks to help you stay organised when you are editing your audio.

Click on the track name. Select 'Name' and type a name for each track.

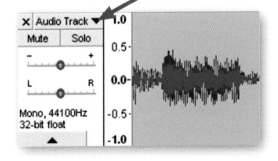

 Test

1 Why is it important to record the audio for your podcast in a quiet place?

2 Explain what the 'Trim' tool is used for in your DAW.

3 Why is it a good idea to record segments of a podcast on separate tracks?

4 Most modern music is made using multi-track recording. Explain some of the benefits of recording music in this way.

5 Multimedia: Make a podcast

In this lesson

You will learn:

▶ how to add a music track to your podcast

▶ how to add effects to your audio tracks

▶ how to mix your final audio.

Add a jingle to your podcast

In your podcast outline in Lesson 5.1, you included a segment of music. This is sometimes called a jingle or 'sting'. It is a short piece of music that the audience will remember.

You can use your DAW to add music files to your podcast. In Audacity, use the 'Import' function.

You can trim and move the music audio. You may need to move the audio on other tracks so they don't play at the same time as the music track.

1 From the 'File' menu select 'Import' and then 'Audio'. Choose a music file.

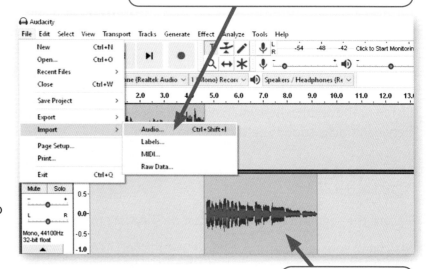

2 The imported audio file will be added as a new track.

Find music and sound effects for podcasts

There are many online libraries of sound effects and music. Make sure the copyright is not owned by someone else. Search online to find copyright-free content. Look for content that has a 'Creative Commons' licence or is described as 'royalty free'. This means you can use the content in your podcasts under certain conditions. The licence will tell you what the conditions of use are.

Remember to include a credit that gives the name of the musician and the pieces of music. For example:

"This podcast features the piece of music 'Raindrops in the forest' by Sajna Begum, which is available under a Creative Commons Attribution-Noncommercial licence."

You can include the credit in your script or in your show notes, if you have created these.

Add effects to audio tracks

Most DAWs have built-in effects that you can use with your tracks and clips. Many effects have **parameters** – settings that control the effects. Use the parameters to customise each effect that you use.

Some effects can make audio clips sound very different so you need to use them carefully. Remember that the listener needs to be able to hear your speech audio clearly.

The table lists some of the most common effects and typical uses.

Effect	Changes it makes	Typical use
Reverb	Adds a 'reverberation' to the audio. This simulates the way sound waves reflect off many surfaces in a room. This effect can make a voice sound as if it is coming from a large room, hall or even a cave.	Can be used with spoken or sung audio to make the sound more natural for the listener. Use with care: very high settings can make the audio difficult to understand.
Echo (or Delay)	Adds an echo by repeating the audio after a short delay. Similar to reverb, but a stronger effect.	Can be used on speech or sound effects to create impact. Use with care: sound can quickly become unclear with too much echo.
Pitch shift	Can raise or lower the pitch of any audio. (The pitch is how high or low the sound is.) Pitch shift can't turn everyone into a great singer though!	Can be used on speech or sound effects for impact or for comedy.
Fade in / Fade out	Fade in: slowly raises the volume from zero at the beginning of a clip. Fade out: slowly lowers the volume of a clip to zero at the end of a clip.	Can be used on any audio to make the join between two clips smoother.

Use effects with care. Make sure your audio is still clear.

Apply the effects

You can apply effects to your audio tracks or to individual clips.

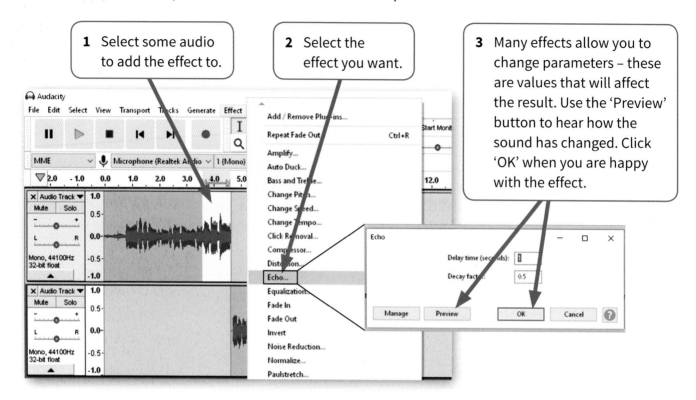

1 Select some audio to add the effect to.

2 Select the effect you want.

3 Many effects allow you to change parameters – these are values that will affect the result. Use the 'Preview' button to hear how the sound has changed. Click 'OK' when you are happy with the effect.

Mix your audio

When you have correctly placed all your clips along the timeline and you have added the effects, you can begin the final stages of your project. The **mixing** stage is when you change the volume level of each track so that the whole podcast sounds right. You need to find the right balance between the volume levels of the different parts of the project: speech, music and sound effects.

To balance the audio volume levels, play the audio and use the 'Gain' sliders to increase or lower the volume of individual tracks until they sound right. Pay particular attention to the transitions between clips and tracks. Most tracks should sound around the same volume level when they are playing.

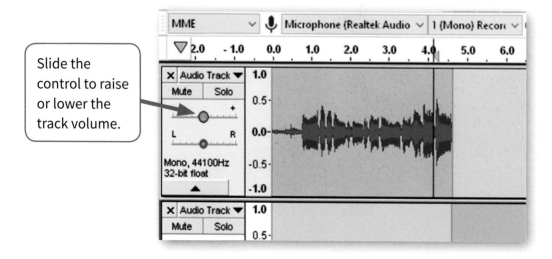

Slide the control to raise or lower the track volume.

 **Activity**

Choose an audio file to add as a jingle to your podcast. Your teacher will help you find files.

Add the jingle in the right place. Use your outline document to remind you where it should go.

Arrange all your audio clips so that each segment flows into the next.

Balance the volume levels of all the tracks so that there are no sudden changes in volume.

Save your work.

 **Extra challenge**

Try adding effects to some parts of your audio clips. For example, try using 'Fade Out' on your jingle.

 **Explore more**

Listen to some jingles on television, radio or the internet. Which are your favourite jingles? Can you explain why you like them?

 Test

1 What is meant by 'mixing' audio tracks?

2 Explain what the 'Fade Out' and 'Fade In' effects do.

3 What do you need to consider when you are adding effects to speech audio in a podcast?

4 Why do you need to add a credit when you use music or other content that is created by someone else?

In this lesson

You will learn:

▶ how to export your project so that you can share it with others

▶ how to write the show notes to go with your podcast

▶ how to design a survey to get feedback

▶ how to add audio files.

Export your project to a sound file

In the last lesson, you finished recording and mixing your podcast pilot episode. Now you are ready to export the project from your DAW software and create a sound file that you can share with others.

It is important to choose your file format carefully. Some formats, such as MP3, use compression to make file sizes smaller. This is good for sharing files. Formats such as WAV use little or no compression. They create big files, but the sound quality can be better. For recordings like podcasts, a compressed format like MP3 is the most common choice.

1 Select the most appropriate audio format.

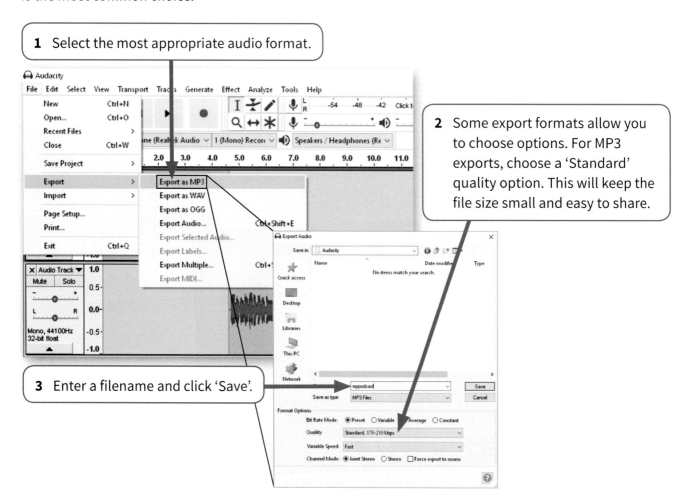

2 Some export formats allow you to choose options. For MP3 exports, choose a 'Standard' quality option. This will keep the file size small and easy to share.

3 Enter a filename and click 'Save'.

Write your show notes

When you share a podcast on the web, you can include notes that give more information and provide more content for your listeners. Podcasters call these notes their 'show notes'. Podcasters usually create a page of show notes for every episode of their podcast.

Show notes can include things like:

▶ links to websites and other content on the web that you mention in your podcast

▶ images of things that you talk about in your podcast

▶ the names of your interview guests and some more information about them.

Use your podcast outline to help you start writing your show notes. You can use the same structure as the outline. Add notes about each segment. It is helpful for your listeners to put the timings in your show notes too, so that they can follow your podcast more easily.

Share your podcast file

Podcasts are usually hosted on websites that specialise in streaming audio. Many listeners use apps called podcatchers to subscribe to podcasts. These apps download the latest episode of a podcast when it is published. This is an example of a podcatcher – you can see the podcasts that the user subscribes to.

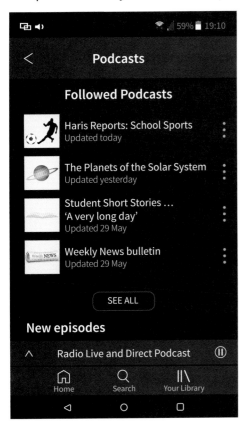

In this unit, you will share your podcast with your classmates using email or a shared drive.

Get feedback on your pilot episode

After you have shared your podcast, ask your audience for feedback. You can design a structured feedback form to help your listeners give you helpful feedback. Include questions about each segment of the podcast, and a box for comments and suggestions.

The feedback will help you improve your pilot podcast. It will also help you make sure the future episodes of your podcast series are of a higher quality and more enjoyable for your audience.

Ask some questions about the content. Use your outline to help you write the questions. For example: "My podcast was aimed at [your audience]. Is the podcast suitable for this audience?" "The aim of my podcast was to [your aim]. Does the podcast meet this aim?" "What was the most interesting part of the podcast?" "How did the podcast make you feel?"

Ask some questions about the style and the technical quality. For example: "Is the presenter speaking clearly?" "Is the presenter speaking too fast or too slow?" "Is there any background noise?"

Can you think of other questions you would like to ask your test listeners?

Here is an example of a feedback form.

Space for the name of the listener who is providing the feedback

Questions about each segment

Podcast title	The School Sports Podcast
Name of reviewer	

Segment	Questions *Please answer the questions about each segment, and add your comments and suggestions in the box.*	
Intro (0:00–0:35)	The aim of this segment is to introduce myself and the subject. ▶ This segment aims to make you feel excited about the podcast. Does it achieve this aim? ▶ Is the presenter speaking clearly? ▶ Is the presenter speaking too fast or too slow? ▶ Is there any background noise?	_____ _____ _____ _____
	Your comments and suggestions:	
Jingle (0:35–0:45)	The aim of the jingle is to be a memorable piece of music that entertains you. ▶ Does it achieve this aim?	_____

Details of each segment, with the timings

Space for the listener's comments and ideas

Collect the feedback from your test listeners so that you can make improvements to your podcast in the next lesson.

 **Activity**

Export your podcast as an audio file. Use a filename that helps listeners remember who made the podcast.

Share your podcast with your classmates. Your teacher will tell you how to do this.

Create a feedback form. Your teacher may give you a form to use.

Listen to some of your classmates' podcasts and fill in the feedback form for each podcast. Your feedback should be honest but helpful and friendly. Aim to help the student improve their podcast.

Collect the feedback forms for your podcast. You will need them in the next lesson.

 **Extra challenge**

Create your show notes. Create a short document with notes about one or more segments. Share your show notes with the classmates who are listening to your podcast.

 Test

1   Name three things you can include in a podcast's show notes to help listeners.
2   Describe at least two ways of sharing your podcast with people.
3   Explain how feedback can help you improve your podcast.
4   Explain the differences between 'compressed' audio and 'uncompressed' audio.

 **Digital citizen of the future**

Asking for feedback is a skill that everyone needs in life. Many people worry that they will receive negative feedback. Feedback on online services and social media can often be 'anonymous' – the person doesn't have to give their name. Sometimes anonymous feedback can be unhelpful and even hurtful.

But getting feedback is one of the best ways to learn and improve. Make sure you get helpful and constructive feedback by carefully choosing the places where you show your work. Use open questions, such as: "What did you like about my work?" Most people will give you honest and helpful feedback when you ask them.

In this lesson

You will learn:

▶ how to analyse the feedback on your podcast episode

▶ how to prioritise work on improvements

▶ how to practise your audio production skills by making improvements to your podcast.

In the last lesson, your classmates gave you some feedback on the pilot episode of your podcast. In this lesson, you will use the skills you have learned in this unit to improve your podcast. You will use the feedback from your classmates to help you.

Analyse feedback and plan improvements

When you analyse the feedback you have received, your aim is to understand what people like and don't like about your work and to decide what you can do to improve it. Start your analysis by reading the feedback forms.

Write down:

▶ your listeners' suggestions for improvements – these are changes you could make.

▶ your listeners comments – turn these into changes that you can make. For example, you can turn the comment "I didn't like the music because it sounded sad" into the suggestion "Use a happier piece of music instead".

Now you will have a list of improvements to make to your podcast. These are your tasks. You need to prioritise the tasks – put them in order of importance.

There are many different ways of prioritising tasks. A good method is to put the tasks in this order:

1 **Most important:** First, fix any big mistakes and technical problems.

2 **Hardest:** Next, make any difficult changes that will take time and effort to do.

3 **Easiest:** Last of all, make smaller and less important changes that are quick to do.

Troubleshoot audio problems

Feedback from your listeners can help you spot problems, but you often have to find the causes of the problems yourself. Finding the causes of problems and then correcting them is called troubleshooting. Troubleshooting is best done methodically – check the possible causes of a problem one by one, until you have found the cause.

Here are some common problems you might need to troubleshoot.

Problem	Possible causes and solutions	Troubleshooting tips
Speech is difficult to hear	**Speech is too quiet in the mix.** Adjust the level (volume) of your audio. If you have music and speech playing at the same time, lower the volume of the music track. **Speech is distorted.** Check the volume of your speech audio and try to reduce it.	If you have many tracks playing at the same time, use the 'Mute' buttons to silence some of them. This makes it easier to hear where the problem is. Use the 'Normalize' tool or effect to smooth out differences in volume.
Sound is distorted	**Digital clipping.** Play back the affected track using the 'Solo' function. If the level meter reaches the red area, clipping might be present. Your DAW may have a tool to remove clipping.	Look for a function or tool such as 'Clip fix' (in Audacity). Try different parameters until your audio sounds clear.
Rumbling sound in the background	**Low frequency rumble** caused by vibrations from air-conditioning, traffic or other movement. You can use an equaliser effect to remove low frequencies.	Try using a 'High pass filter' effect and set the frequency parameter to around 80–120Hz.

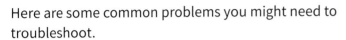

Use a shock mount for your microphone to reduce low-frequency rumble.

Make improvements to your podcast

Open your DAW project file. Make a **safety copy** of your project by saving it with a different name. You can add the word 'edit' to the end of the filename, for example. If you make any mistakes during the editing, you can return to the safety copy and start again.

Now you can begin making your changes. Start with the highest-priority change.

You can look again at Lessons 5.3 and 5.4 to find instructions on how to edit your audio.

To move tracks along the timeline, look at Lesson 5.3.

To trim a clip to shorten it, look at Lesson 5.3.

To add an effect to a clip, look at Lesson 5.4.

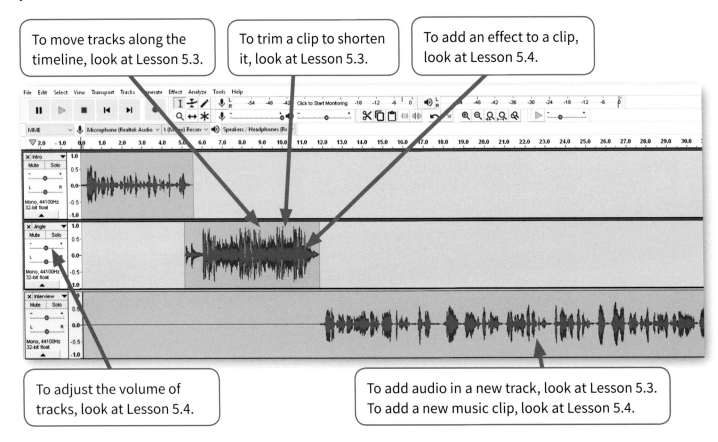

To adjust the volume of tracks, look at Lesson 5.4.

To add audio in a new track, look at Lesson 5.3.
To add a new music clip, look at Lesson 5.4.

 Activity

Analyse the feedback for your podcast episode.

Write down a prioritised list of changes to make.

Make the changes in order of priority.

Save your work. You have completed your podcast pilot episode.

Extra challenge

Listen back to your completed podcast. Do you think that it is better after the changes you have made? Do you think your changes will please the listeners who gave the feedback? Write down how your changes have made a difference.

Do you want to learn more about digital audio?

Podcasting is a great way to start working with digital audio. You can record and share a podcast with very little experience and no specialist equipment. Once you have learned how to connect a microphone and use a DAW, you can try new things.

Next-level podcasting

Search the web for ideas about advancing your podcasting skills.

▶ Set up a home studio. Use a condenser microphone and a mixer to improve the quality. Experiment with home-made soundproofing to make your audio recordings clearer and more professional.

▶ Use an audio chat service to record your podcast with friends and family around the world.

▶ Promote your podcast using a podcast hosting service.

Move into music

Do you play a musical instrument? Or love to sing? Use a search engine to find out more about these options:

▶ Use your DAW to record music. Multi-track audio allows you to play and sing like a professional.

▶ Find royalty-free backing tracks and record your voice and instruments over the backing tracks.

▶ Share your music using a streaming platform.

 Test

1 What does 'troubleshooting' mean?

2 What is the purpose of a 'safety copy' of a file?

3 After analysing your feedback, which of these problems should you fix first?

   a the easiest   b the hardest   c the most important

4 Describe how you decided on the priority of the problems or changes to your podcast.

You have learned

▶ how to plan a podcast by creating an outline and script

▶ how to record digital audio using your computer

▶ how to edit and improve digital audio recordings using digital audio workstation (DAW) software

▶ how to use feedback to improve your podcast.

Try the test and activity. They will help you to see how much you understand.

Test

1 Describe the main functions of a DAW.

2 What does the word 'feedback' mean?

3 Explain the term 'multi-track recording'.

4 Put these planning stages in the right order: write the outline, write the script, write down the aim, discuss ideas.

5 Describe at least one way that you used feedback from your audience to improve your podcast pilot episode.

6 Name three common audio effects that you can add to a recording when you are using a DAW.

 Activity

Download the 'Techpodcast' audio files.

You are the audio production engineer at Podcast Production Services, a small company that helps podcasters produce their programmes. A podcast director has asked you to create a podcast from some prerecorded audio files.

The director has given you these instructions for the running order. They have also made suggestions for some segments:

Segment	Content	Suggestions
1	Intro (presenter); use file techpodcast_intro.wav	
2	Jingle (music); use file techpodcast_jingle.wav	You could use Fade Out at the end of the jingle.
3	Interview (presenter and interviewee); use file techpodcast_intervew.wav	Please trim silence at the beginning of the clip.
4	Outro (presenter); use file techpodcast_outro.wav	

Open your DAW and import each of the clips in a separate track.

Arrange the clips in the correct running order.

Make the suggested changes to the clips, and any other changes that you think are needed. Check that they are still in order and have no long breaks between them.

Save your project.

Export your podcast to an audio file.

Self-evaluation

- I answered test questions 1 and 2.
- I started the activity. I imported some audio clips into my DAW and started to arrange them.
- I answered test questions 1–4.
- I made good progress in the activity. I arranged all the clips in the correct order.
- I answered all the test questions.
- I finished the activity. I edited the clips and exported the podcast to an audio file.

Re-read any parts of the unit you feel unsure about. Try the test and activity again – can you do more this time?

6 Numbers and data: Business data table

You will learn

▶ how to store data in a data table so people can access and use the data

▶ how to generate useful business information from a computer data table

▶ how to use error checks and error messages to block bad data.

In this unit you will make a simple one-table database for use in a business. You will invent an internet shopping business which sells goods online. You will create a data table for your business to record the items that you have in stock.

🔌 Unplugged

Working in a small group, develop an idea for an internet shopping business. On paper, make a design for the website and a list of what you could sell. Design a logo and a slogan for your business.

Talk about...

Do you or your family use online shopping to buy goods? Which do you prefer – shopping online or going to the shops? What are the advantages and disadvantages of each type of shopping?

Learning outcomes: Create a single-table data file; Check data input for accuracy

Digital citizen of the future

The growth of online shopping has affected modern town centres and local shopping centres. Fewer people visit the shops. Some shops have closed.

Is it important to support local shops? How can we help to support shops in our local area? Will changes in shopping affect the jobs that are available in your community? These are important questions for citizens of the future.

Did you know?

Jeff Bezos created the online shopping website Amazon in 1994. The internet was very new at the time. Jeff Bezos decided to make a website to sell things. He wrote a list of 20 products he might sell. In the end, he decided that his new business would sell books, because there is worldwide interest in reading books.

Jeff Bezos called his company Amazon because the Amazon River is the biggest river in the world, and he planned to make his online store the biggest in the world.

atomic

AutoSum   currency   data table

field   information   key field

record   validation

In this lesson

You will learn:

▶ how to select and collect data for a business

▶ how to create your own unique business idea.

Spiral back

In Student Book 6 you created a spreadsheet table with business data. In this lesson you will collect data about a business idea. In the following lessons you will use your data to make a table of useful business data. Your work in this unit will be unique to you.

Choose a business idea

In Unit 2 you learned about using online shopping to buy and sell things on the internet. In this unit you will imagine that you are starting an online store. You will use a spreadsheet to keep the records for your online business.

First, you must decide what you will sell in your online store. You will see the work of a student called Janna in this unit. Janna decided her online store would sell homemade jam. You will choose a different type of product to sell. You will use the names of real products.

The students at City Park School had a discussion. They talked about their business ideas. They talked about products that they would like to sell. Here are some of the business ideas that the students chose:

▶ selling trainers

▶ selling mobile phones

▶ selling dressmaking supplies.

 **Activity**

Think about your online business idea now. Choose an idea you are interested in. Talk about your idea with other students in your class. Then write down your idea and a name for your business.

Research products to sell

Now you need to choose the products you will sell in your online store. Your customers will want to know more than just the name of your products. You will need to find out facts about the products so you can provide useful information for your customers.

Internet research

To find out facts about products, you will carry out internet research.

You must find web pages with the information you need.

▶ Use a search engine to find web pages with products that are appropriate for your business idea.

▶ Find out facts about each product you want to sell.

For example, Amrit decided to sell trainers and other sports shoes. He typed 'buy trainers' into a search engine.

Some of the results of your search will be links to adverts. In this task it is OK to look at adverts. Adverts will give you ideas for products that you could sell.

Spiral back

 You have learned about internet searching in Unit 2 of the books in this series. Now you will use your online research skills to find information about products you will sell in your business.

Web pages

Amrit found a web page with information about trainers. The website had pictures of the trainers, and other facts about the trainers.

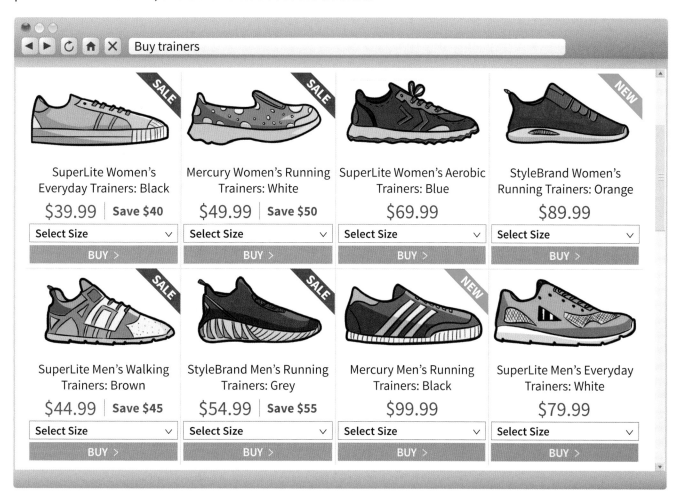

You can click on any of the products to find out more facts. In this task you are just collecting facts – you don't need to collect any images.

Choose products

Make sure you look at several web pages and lots of products in your research. Choose 10 different products that you want to sell. They don't all have to be made by the same company. They don't all have to be on the same web page.

Write down the names of the products you want to sell in your online shop and the names of the websites where you found them.

Choose the facts

What facts should you store about each product in your spreadsheet? What will your customers want to know?

The facts that Janna will store in her spreadsheet of jam products are shown on the right.

Whatever products you choose, you will probably need these facts:

▶ name of the product

▶ cost of the product

▶ the company that makes the product (the supplier).

You will also need some facts that are special to your product. People buying jam will want to know the flavour of the jam and the weight of the jam in each jar. People buying trainers will want to know the colour and the shoe size. People buying mobile phones will want to know the storage capacity and screen size.

Flavour: Strawberry

Weight: 300g

Brand: Best-buy jam

Supplier: Market Foods Ltd

Cost: $4.99

Collect data

There are several ways to collect the data that you need.

▶ You can look at the website and make notes on paper. Then create a new document in your word-processing software and type up your notes.

On the right are some example notes that Janna made about some jam products. Janna typed the data into a word-processed document.

▶ You can have two windows open on your computer at the same time:

• one window with the web page of data

• one window with the word-processed document.

You can type your notes straight into the document. You can also copy and paste data from the website into the document.

Product notes

Best-buy Strawberry
$4.99 for 300g
Supplier - Market Foods Ltd

Organic Plum
$7.99 for 500g
Supplier - Homemade Preserves

Organic Cherry
$9.99 for 300g
Supplier - Homemade Preserves

Here are some example notes that Amrit made about trainers to sell in his online store. He used a split screen, with the web data on one side of the screen and his word-processed document on the other side of the screen.

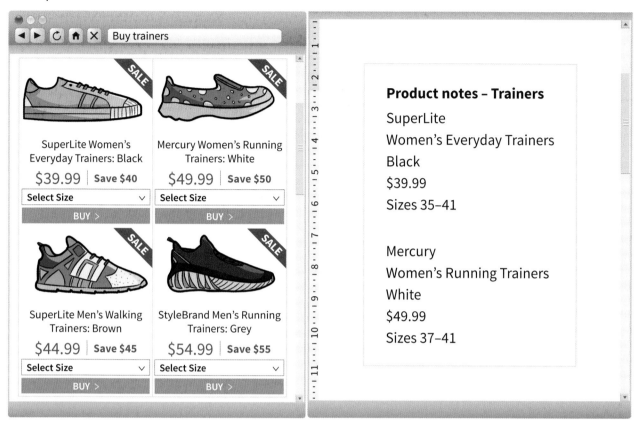

 **Activity**

Decide what products you will sell in your online business.

Carry out internet research to find lots of different examples of this product.

Choose 10 products to sell in your business.

Decide which facts you will collect about your products – at least four facts.

Collect the facts in a word-processed document.

 **Extra challenge**

You have collected and stored data about products. What other facts might a business need as well as product data? Make brief notes on other facts that the owner of an online shopping business might need.

 **Be creative**

Design a logo for your business. You can draw it, paint it or create it using a graphics application.

 Test

1 Write a list of the products you have decided to sell in your online store.

2 Write three facts you have collected about your products.

3 State why each fact is useful to your business or to your customers.

4 Give the URLs of the websites that you used in this lesson.

In this lesson

You will learn:

▶ the difference between data and information

▶ how to make a data table by organising data into records and fields.

Data and information

Two important terms in computing are **data** and **information**:

▶ Data means facts and figures. In the last lesson you collected data about products for your new business.

▶ Information is data that has been organised. Organising data makes it more useful.

The task of turning data into information is sometimes called **data processing**. Data processing is one of the most important things that people do with computers. We input facts into the computer, then we organise the facts to make them more useful.

In this lesson you will organise product data to make it more useful. You will organise the data into a table. Organising data in a table has several advantages:

▶ It will be easier to find the information you want.

▶ It will be easier to create extra information, for example, using calculations.

▶ It will be easier to spot mistakes and fix them.

Data table

At the moment, your product data is stored in a word-processed document. This document is not very useful for running a business. It will be difficult to find the facts you want. To make the product data more useful, you will organise the data into a **data table**.

A data table is a grid of rows and columns. Each cell of the data table holds a single item of data. The data items are organised to make it easy to find the facts you want.

A lot of the data we see in everyday life is organised as data tables. Here are some examples:

▶ the register that your teacher fills in at the start of a lesson

▶ a price list in a restaurant

▶ a board at an airport showing departures.

In each case, the information is organised into rows and columns to make a table. In this unit you will use spreadsheet software to make a table of product data.

Records and fields

A data table is made of **records** and **fields**.

▶ A record stores all the information about one item. The rows of a table are records.

▶ A field stores one type of data. The columns of a table are fields.

Every record in a data table has the same columns. That means you store the same type of information about each item. Look at the data you collected in the last lesson. What type of information have you collected? Make a list. For example:

▶ product name or brand

▶ colour

▶ size.

When you have made a list of the type of information you want to store, you are ready to start making the data table.

Colour: Yellow   **Size:** 43

Brand: SuperLite   **Supplier:** Maxx Sports

Cost: $79.99

Make a spreadsheet table

You are going to organise your product data into fields and records. You will use spreadsheet software.

Look at the list that says what information you want to store. Each item of information will be a field of your data table. Each field has a name. The name of the field tells you what information is stored in that field. The field names go along the top of the spreadsheet – one in each column.

Now look at your word-processed document where you have stored the data that you collected. This data goes into the spreadsheet – one fact in each field.

This picture shows the data for Janna's online jam shop. Janna has organised the data into records and fields.

	A	B	C	D	E
1	Flavour	Weight	Brand	Supplier	Cost
2	Strawberry	300g	Best-buy	Market Foods Ltd	$4.99
3	Plum	500g	Organic	Homemade Preserves	$7.99
4	Cherry	300g	Organic	Homemade Preserves	$9.99
5	Strawberry	350g	Low-sugar	Homemade Preserves	$9.99
6	Raspberry	300g	Finest	Handmade Jam	$11.99
7	Blueberry	400g	Finest	Handmade Jam	$12.99
8	Mixed Fruit	350g	Best-buy	Hungry Farmer Jam Company	$7.50
9	Plum	500g	Low-sugar	Hungry Farmer Jam Company	$7.50
10	Strawberry	400g	Organic	Market Foods Ltd	$4.50
11	Cherry	300g	Finest	Luxury Jam	$19.99
12					

Each spreadsheet row is a record.

Each spreadsheet column is a field.

Key fields

A customer to the Janna's online jam shop needs to be able to identify the exact product that they want to buy. How can they do this?

▶ Not by flavour: There is more than one jam with each flavour. For example, there are three different strawberry products.

▶ Not by brand: There is more than one jam of each brand. For example, there are two different Best-buy products.

▶ Not by supplier: There is more than one jam from each supplier. For example, there are two different Handmade Jam products.

For this reason, a data table needs one extra field. This extra field is called the **key field**. The key field stores a piece of data that is unique – the data is different for each record. The key field is used to identify the record. Another name for the key field is the primary key.

Insert a new column

The key field usually goes in column A. So you need to make room for it. An easy way to do this is to insert a new column.

▶ Select column A – click on the letter A at the top of the column.

▶ Click on the Insert button at the top right of the screen. Select 'Insert Sheet Columns' from the menu.

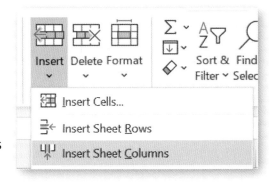

A new empty column A appears. None of your old data is lost. It has just moved one column to the right.

Add a product code

Now you can enter key field data for each product.

A code makes a good key field. The person designing the data table will give each item a different code. For example, in a table of products, each item will have a product code. The code can be made of characters or numbers.

Think of a code for each product in your data table. Janna gave her products codes that begin with the letter P (for product) and then a unique number.

	A	B	C	D	E	F
1	Product code	Flavour	Weight	Brand	Supplier	Cost
2	P0001	Strawberry	300g	Best-buy	Market Foods Ltd	$4.99
3	P0002	Plum	500g	Organic	Homemade Preserves	$7.99
4	P0003	Cherry	300g	Organic	Homemade Preserves	$9.99
5	P0004	Strawberry	350g	Low-sugar	Homemade Preserves	$9.99
6	P0005	Raspberry	300g	Finest	Handmade Jam	$11.99
7	P0006	Blueberry	400g	Finest	Handmade Jam	$12.99
8	P0007	Mixed Fruit	350g	Best-buy	Hungry Farmer Jam Company	$7.50
9	P0008	Plum	500g	Low-sugar	Hungry Farmer Jam Company	$7.50
10	P0009	Strawberry	400g	Organic	Market Foods Ltd	$4.50
11	P0010	Cherry	300g	Finest	Luxury Jam	$19.99

The key field is usually the first field in the data table.

 **Activity**

Make a data table using your product data.

▶ Enter field names as column headings.

▶ Enter the product data, with the data for each product in one row.

▶ Create a key field and enter the product code for each product.

Atomic facts

In a data table, the facts should be **atomic**. The word 'atomic' has a special meaning when you are working with data. It means that you cannot split up the data into smaller parts. Here are two examples:

Best-buy Strawberry 300g

> This data is not atomic.
>
> You can split this data up. You need to turn it into three fields:
>
> ▶ Best-buy
> ▶ Strawberry
> ▶ 300g

Market Foods Ltd

> This data is atomic.
>
> Although the data is made of three words, you cannot split them up any further. The words identify a single fact – the name of the supplier. The word 'Market' on its own would not make sense in this data table.

 Extra challenge

Make sure all the data in your data table is atomic.

✓ **Test**

1 What information is shown in the top row of a data table?

2 Write a definition of a data record. What part of a data table is used to store one record?

3 What is the purpose of a key field in a data table?

4 Data fields should be atomic. Explain what this means.

In this lesson

You will learn:

▶ how to choose the right data type for each field in the table.

Your data

You have stored data in a data table.

▶ Each fact is stored in one field of the data table. The fields are the columns of the table. Your table should have at least five columns (including the key field).

▶ All the information about one product is stored in a record of the data table. The records are the rows of the table. Your table should have at least 10 rows.

Now you will improve the data table and make it more useful.

Data types

In Unit 1 you learned how different types of data are stored in the computer. When you made a program in Unit 3 you learned about different data types.

Data types in Python

In Python, every variable has a data type. The data types you have used in Python are:

▶ String variables: hold text values. The computer holds this data using ASCII values. ASCII data cannot be used in calculations.

▶ Integer variables: hold whole numbers only

▶ Float variables: can hold any number, including decimal values.

Data types in a data table

Data tables also use data types. The data stored in each field of a data table has a data type. All the data in one column should be the same data type.

Two important data types used in data tables are:

▶ Text data: cannot be used in calculations

▶ Number values: can be used in calculations.

Text data

Some cells in your data table store text data. Text data can include any character that you can type with the keyboard. Here are some examples of spreadsheet cells that hold text data.

L
Product code
P0001
Total cost
$4.50
Weight = 500g

Text data is **left-aligned**. That means the data appears at the left of the cell. Any empty space is shown on the right of the cell.

Some data in your table will be used in calculations. If you think data will be used in calculations it must not be stored as text data. It must be stored as a number value.

Number values

Number values represent a quantity or amount of something. Number values are shown using the digits from 0 to 9. Numbers might include the decimal point or the negative sign. Remember that number values cannot include other characters such as commas, currency symbols or letters of the alphabet.

Which are numbers?

Look at this image. Which of these spreadsheet cells store number values?

It is quite easy to spot the number values. Number values are **right-aligned**. That means the data appears at the right of the cell. Any empty space is shown on the left of the cell.

L
Product code
P0001
Total cost
4.50
500

Remove text characters

Your data table should include some numerical data. For example:

▶ the size or weight of a product

▶ the cost of a product.

You must make sure that this data is stored using number values. Check to see if these fields include any non-numerical characters. Take out those extra characters.

Weights

Janna's table included the weight of each product. Janna had input the weight as '300g' or '400g'. These are text values because they include the letter 'g'. The g stands for 'grams'.

But weight should be stored as a number value because it represents a quantity. Janna had to change this data into a number value. She deleted the 'g' from each cell. This left just the number value. For example, '300'.

Janna put the letter 'g' into the field name instead. That was to remind her that the values stood for weight in grams. The new field name was: **Weight (g)**.

Money values

Janna's table also included the cost of each product. The values in this field are amounts of money so they are number data. But Janna had input this data with the currency symbol $. She had to delete the currency symbol. If you have included other symbols, such as a comma, delete these too.

Here is what Janna's jam table looked like after she had removed the extra characters from the numerical data. You can see that the number data is right-aligned. That showed Janna that she had entered the data correctly.

	A	B	C	D	E	F
1	Flavour	Weight (g)	Brand	Supplier	Cost	
2	Strawberry	300	Best-buy	Market Foods Ltd	4.99	
3	Plum	500	Organic	Homemade Preserves	7.99	
4	Cherry	300	Organic	Homemade Preserves	9.99	
5	Strawberry	350	Low-sugar	Homemade Preserves	9.99	
6	Raspberry	300	Finest	Handmade Jam	11.99	
7	Blueberry	400	Finest	Handmade Jam	12.99	
8	Mixed Fruit	350	Best-buy	Hungry Farmer Jam Company	7.5	

Number formats

Data format means the style used to display data. You must choose a suitable format for each field in the data table. Every data value in a field is the same type of data so it must have the same format.

Some of the data formats that are available are shown in the tool bar at the top of the spreadsheet.

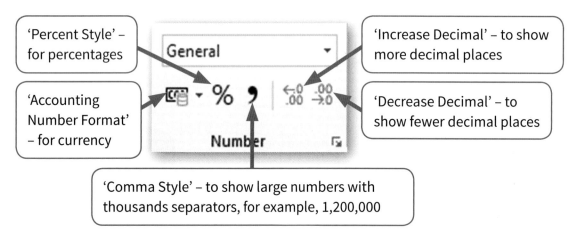

'Percent Style' – for percentages

'Accounting Number Format' – for currency

'Increase Decimal' – to show more decimal places

'Decrease Decimal' – to show fewer decimal places

'Comma Style' – to show large numbers with thousands separators, for example, 1,200,000

Choosing currency format

Currency means a money value. The icon for currency format is a picture of some money. In Janna's data table, column F holds the product cost. This data is a currency value, so Janna decided to format column F as currency data.

▶ Janna clicked on the letter 'F' to select the whole column.

▶ Then she clicked on the currency icon.

Clicking on the currency button opens a menu. You can use it to choose a currency symbol for your product costs.

£ English (United Kingdom)
$ English (United States)
€ Euro (€ 123)
More Accounting Formats...

Format as a table

Spreadsheet software allows you to format data as a table. Formatting as a table will make it easier for you to work with your data. For example, it will be easy to sort or search the data. It will be easy to enter calculations. Select all the data you have entered, including the field names.

Find the button on the tool bar that says 'Format as Table'. Select this button and choose a colour and style for your table.

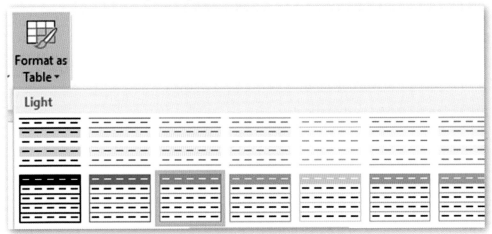

Your completed data table will look something like this.

	A Product code	B Flavour	C Weight (g)	D Brand	E Supplier	F Cost
2	P0001	Strawberry	300	Best-buy	Market Foods Ltd	$ 4.99
3	P0002	Plum	500	Organic	Homemade Preserves	$ 7.99
4	P0003	Cherry	300	Organic	Homemade Preserves	$ 9.99
5	P0004	Strawberry	350	Low-sugar	Homemade Preserves	$ 9.99
6	P0005	Raspberry	300	Finest	Handmade Jam	$ 11.99
7	P0006	Blueberry	400	Finest	Handmade Jam	$ 12.99
8	P0007	Mixed Fruit	350	Best-buy	Hungry Farmer Jam Company	$ 7.50
9	P0008	Plum	500	Low-sugar	Hungry Farmer Jam Company	$ 7.50
10	P0009	Strawberry	400	Organic	Market Foods Ltd	$ 4.50
11	P0010	Cherry	300	Finest	Luxury Jam	$ 19.99

 **Activity**

Make your spreadsheet of products into a data table. Make sure you:

▶ identify all the fields with numerical data – remove letters and other symbols from this data

▶ format money values as currency

▶ format the whole spreadsheet as a table.

 **Extra challenge**

You can change the style and colour of your spreadsheet table. Try a few different styles. Choose a style that is right for your business.

 Test

1 Which statement is true?

a All data in one record should be the same data type.

b All data in one field should be the same data type.

2 When you look at a field you can tell if it stores a number value or text data. How can you tell?

3 How is text data stored in the computer?

4 You cannot do some actions using text data – give an example.

In this lesson

You will learn:

▶ how to use calculations to generate business information.

Number values and calculations

In this lesson you will use calculations to extend your data table. You will do calculations using spreadsheet formulas. You will calculate:

▶ the number of items in stock at the start and end of the day

▶ the value of your stock.

You will learn how to choose and use the right calculations for business purposes.

Items in stock

Stock is a business term. It means all the items that the business owns. It can include:

▶ products for sale

▶ raw materials and items being made in the business

▶ other things the business owns, such as tools.

It is very important for a business to keep track of the number of items they have in stock. Stock represents a big investment for almost all businesses. The list of all the items a business has in stock is often called the inventory.

Stock check

How does a business know how many items it has in stock? Workers in the company carry out a stock check. That means they go to the stockroom or warehouse and count all the items. Nowadays, the worker who carries out the stock check can use an inventory on a portable device such as a tablet.

Sometimes stock is marked with bar codes. The worker can scan the code. This method is quicker and more accurate.

The stock check tells the business the number of each item it has on that day. But the number of items will change from day to day:

▶ **Stock in:** The business may buy items from suppliers. Customers may return items. The number of items in stock goes up.

▶ **Stock out:** The business may sell items. Sometimes items are lost or broken. The number of items in stock goes down.

The business needs to adjust its inventory when stock comes in and when stock goes out. This allows the business to keep track of the number of items in stock.

Opening and closing stock

Now you will add four new fields to your data table so you can record stock:

▶ **Opening stock:** This is the number of items in stock to begin with (for example, at the start of a day). The workers get this number by counting the items.

▶ **Stock in:** This is the number of items that come into the warehouse. The workers get this number by recording all the items that come in during the day.

▶ **Stock out:** This is the number of items that go out of the warehouse. The workers get this number by recording all the items that leave the warehouse.

▶ **Closing stock:** This is calculated from opening stock by adding stock in and subtracting stock out.

Add these four fields to your data table.

Add stock figures to your data table

Your stock isn't real! That means you cannot do a real stock check.

▶ Make up a number for the 'Opening stock' for each product.

▶ Enter '0' in the 'Stock in' and 'Stock out' columns for now.

▶ Leave the 'Closing stock' field empty for now.

Janna added these four fields to her jam table. It looked like this:

F Cost	G Opening stock	H Stock in	I Stock out	J Closing stock
$ 4.99	700	0	0	
$ 7.99	800	0	0	
$ 9.99	70	0	0	
$ 9.99	900	0	0	
$ 11.99	1200	0	0	
$ 12.99	500	0	0	
$ 7.50	400	0	0	
$ 7.50	700	0	0	
$ 4.50	800	0	0	
$ 19.99	800	0	0	

Calculate closing stock

In the last lesson you formatted your data as a table. The table format is very helpful when you want to do calculations because you only need to enter a calculation once, at the top of a column. The computer will work out the correct answer for every row of the data table.

You will calculate the amount of closing stock. The calculation is:

'Opening stock' ADD 'Stock in' SUBTRACT 'Stock out'

Follow these steps:

▶ Click on the cell below the column heading in the 'Closing stock' column.

▶ Type an equals sign to start the formula.

▶ Click on the 'Opening stock' cell in the same row.

▶ Type an ADD sign (+) and click on the 'Stock in' cell in the same row.

▶ Type a SUBTRACT sign (-) and click on the 'Stock out' cell in the same row.

Janna entered this formula in her data table:

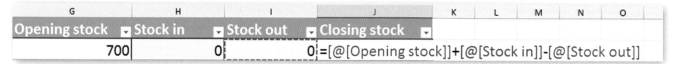

G	H	I	J	K	L	M	N	O
Opening stock	Stock in	Stock out	Closing stock					
700	0	0	=[@[Opening stock]]+[@[Stock in]]-[@[Stock out]]					

Press the 'Enter' key and the computer will work out the closing stock. It will work out the correct answer for every product in the table. If you make a mistake with the formula, just start again.

 **Activity**

Make up some values for the 'Opening stock', 'Stock in' and 'Stock out' columns for every item in your inventory. Enter these values in your data table.

Enter a formula to calculate the closing stock.

Stock value

Businesses spend a lot of money on buying stock so they need to know the value of their stock. The stock value is the value of each item multiplied by the number of items in stock. You will use the spreadsheet to calculate this value.

Find the next empty column in your data table. Type 'Stock value' at the top of the column. The column is added to your data table automatically.

Calculate stock value

Now add a calculation to work out stock value:

'Closing stock' MULTIPLIED BY 'Cost'

Use your spreadsheet skills to enter this formula. Remember that the * symbol means 'multiply'.

Janna entered this 'Stock value' formula in column K of her table:

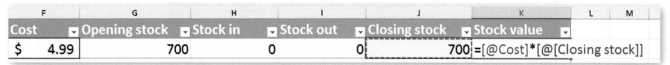

	F	G	H	I	J	K	L	M
	Cost	Opening stock	Stock in	Stock out	Closing stock	Stock value		
	$ 4.99	700	0	0	700	=[@Cost]*[@[Closing stock]]		

Press the 'Enter' key. The stock value will appear in every row of your table. The data in this column is a currency value so change it to currency format.

Total stock value

In maths, to sum means to add up a series of values. Spreadsheets provide a useful function called **AutoSum**. AutoSum adds up all the values in a field. You can only use AutoSum if the column holds number values.

Find the AutoSum button on the right-hand side of the tool bar. It looks like this:

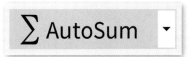

$\sum$ AutoSum

Select the first empty cell at the bottom of the 'Stock value' column. Then click on the AutoSum button. Your spreadsheet will show the total value of all the stock.

The image on the right shows the 'Stock value' column in Janna's table. Your numbers will be different.

K
Stock value
$ 3,343.30
$ 6,951.30
$ 799.20
$ 10,519.47
$ 7,194.00
$ 3,637.20
$ 2,775.00
$ 4,425.00
$ 1,800.00
$ 6,996.50
$ 48,440.97

Extra challenge

Enter spreadsheet formulas to:

▶ calculate the stock value for each product

▶ calculate the total stock value for your business.

Test

1   A warehouse worker uses a tablet to do her job. Write down one thing she might use the tablet for.

2   What does 'opening stock' mean? How do businesses find out the quantity of their opening stock?

3   In your own words, explain how to calculate closing stock.

4   How can you calculate the total value of all the stock that a business has?

In this lesson

You will learn:

▶ how to use validation to find mistakes in your data table.

Missing stock

In the last lesson you calculated the closing stock for your online business. The closing stock tells you how many items should be in the warehouse. Sometimes the number of items in the warehouse does not match the closing stock number. There are many reasons for this:

▶ The count during the last stock check was wrong.

▶ Workers have not recorded stock changes (stock in and out) correctly.

▶ Workers have put items back in the wrong place.

▶ Some items may have been broken or stolen.

It is bad for a business when stock is missing. Mistakes in recording stock data can cost money and cause problems. The bigger the business and the more stock it has, the more likely it is that there will be errors in the stock data.

Every business needs to have accurate data about its inventory. Good stock records will help.

Validation

Validation is a way of checking data. Validation uses rules to check the data. There are two types of data validation:

▶ Validation of data that is already in the data table: If the data breaks the rules, it is highlighted so you can find and change it. You will use this method in this lesson.

▶ Validation of data entry: If the data breaks the rules, you cannot enter it in the data table. You will use this method in the next lesson.

Data that does not obey validation rules is called 'invalid' data. You pronounce this word with the stress on the second syllable: 'in-VAL-id'.

Validation rules

Validation can use rules like these to check that data is accurate:

▶ the type of data (text, number etc.) – for example, text for product name, number for opening stock, etc.

- the range of number values – for example, only values between 0.99 and 9.99 are allowed

- a list of 'allowed' data – for example, a list of the brands stocked.

Validation rules for stock

In a business, the warehouse workers will input the number of items in stock and the number of stock items that come in and go out. The validation rules will make sure that they only enter valid data. How do you decide which validation rules to use?

Think of the online jam business. When a worker enters the number of jars of jam in stock, the input must obey these rules:

- It must be a number – you cannot have 'z' jars of jam.

- It must be a whole number – you cannot have 0.5 jars of jam.

- It must be a number greater than or equal to 0 – you cannot have –20 jars of jam.

Do these rules apply to the products in your business too?

Find bad data

Bad data is data that contains errors. It is important to check the data in the data table for errors. In your business there are only 10 records. But in a real business there might be thousands or even millions of records. Businesses can use validation rules to find errors hidden in all their data.

Make a deliberate mistake

You can add deliberate mistakes in your data to check that your validation rules work. When you add the validation rules, they should find your deliberate mistakes.

Janna made two deliberate mistakes to check her validation rules. She changed the 'Opening stock' for product P0003 to –70. She changed the 'Stock in' for product P0004 to 2.33. Here is the table with the deliberate mistakes.

	G		H		I		J	
Opening stock		Stock in		Stock out		Closing stock		
700		20		50		670		
800		70		0		870		
-70		90		80		-60		
900		2.33		80		822.33		
1200		400		1000		600		
500		30		250		280		
400		60		90		370		
700		90		200		590		
800		100		500		400		
800		150		600		350		

Make sure your data has some deliberate mistakes too. Now you will use validation rules to find these mistakes.

Select cells to validate

Select all the cells where you want to apply the validation rules. To find the deliberate mistakes in this example, you need to check the cells that show:

► Opening stock   ► Stock in   ► Stock out.

Select these cells. Do not include the column headers. Here is Janna's spreadsheet with these cells selected.

Supplier	Cost	Opening stock	Stock in	Stock out	Closing stock	Stock value
Market Foods Ltd	$ 4.99	700	20	50	670	$ 3,343.30
Homemade Preserves	$ 7.99	800	70	0	870	$ 6,951.30
Homemade Preserves	$ 9.99	-70	90	80	-60	$ -599.40
Homemade Preserves	$ 9.99	900	2.33	80	822.33	$ 8,215.08
Handmade Jam	$ 11.99	1200	400	1000	600	$ 7,194.00
Handmade Jam	$ 12.99	500	30	250	280	$ 3,637.20
Hungry Farmer Jam Company	$ 7.50	400	60	90	370	$ 2,775.00
Hungry Farmer Jam Company	$ 7.50	700	90	200	590	$ 4,425.00
Market Foods Ltd	$ 4.50	800	100	500	400	$ 1,800.00
Luxury Jam	$ 19.99	800	150	600	350	$ 6,996.50
						$ 44,737.98

Start validation

Open the 'Data' tool bar at the top of the screen. Find the button that says 'Data Validation'.

Click on the icon. You will see a new window. This is where you enter the validation rules.

Data Validation ▼

Data Tools

Set the validation rules

You will choose from the drop-down menus to set your validation rules. Remember that the data values in the selected columns must be whole numbers. Find 'Whole number' in the first drop-down menu.

The values must be 0 or more (no negative numbers). Find 'greater than or equal to' in the next drop-down menu. Type '0' for the minimum value.

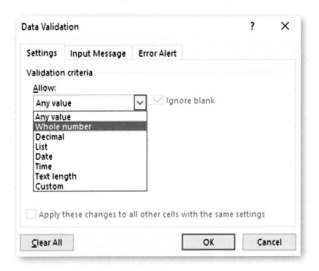

Now you have set all the validation rules for the fields where the warehouse workers will enter stock numbers.

Circle errors

Remember that in real life your data table might have thousands or even millions of records. The computer can help you find all the records that break the validation rules.

Go back to the 'Data Validation' icon. Click on the arrow to open a menu. Select 'Circle Invalid Data'.

The software draws a red circle round all the invalid data. Remember: invalid data is data that breaks the validation rules you have set.

Here is Janna's spreadsheet. The computer has found and circled the errors.

Opening stock	Stock in	Stock out
700	20	50
800	70	0
-70	90	80
900	2.33	80
1200	400	1000
500	30	250
400	60	90
700	90	200
800	100	500
800	150	600

Now you can find and fix the mistakes in your spreadsheet.

Enter some bad data (deliberate mistakes) into your data table.

Set validation rules and tell the software to circle the errors.

Fix the deliberate mistakes.

The data in the 'Cost' field must be a number value. It must be greater than 0. However, it should be a decimal value rather than a whole number. Use the skills you have learned to add a validation check to the 'Cost' field.

1 What is the name for using rules to check data?

2 Explain why the 'Opening stock' field must have integer (whole number) data only.

3 Explain why the data in the 'Stock in' column must be greater than or equal to 0.

4 What validation rules would you use for the data in the 'Cost' field?

In this lesson

You will learn:

▶ how to use validation to block bad input to your data table

▶ how to use error messages to help the user enter valid data.

Block invalid data input

In the last lesson you set some validation rules. These checks found bad data in the table.

Validation rules do another useful thing. They stop the user from entering bad data into the table. The validation rules that you set in the last lesson will block bad input. Test it for yourself:

▶ Try to input a negative number anywhere in the 'Opening stock', 'Stock in' or 'Stock out' columns.

▶ Try to enter any other data that breaks the validation rules. For example, try to enter a letter or a number with a decimal point.

You will see an error message. It appears in a message box like this.

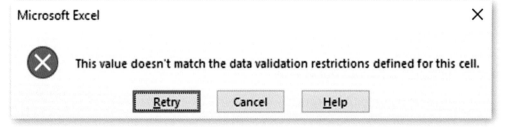

If you do not see an error message, the validation check is not working. Go back to the last lesson and enter the validation check again.

 **Activity**

Try to input bad data into the table and see what happens.

Improve the error message

In Units 3 and 4 you learned that error messages are useful. A program error message helps you to find and fix errors when you are programming. An error message tells you:

▶ where the mistake is

▶ what the mistake is.

Think about the error messages you saw when you were making Python programs. Which ones were most useful? What error messages would you like to see in your data table?

What makes a useful error message?

A validation error message should be useful. It should stop the user from entering bad data. It should help the user to enter valid data. The message should tell the user:

▶ that the input they just entered is invalid

▶ what input they should enter instead.

Look at the error message box on page 166. The box has a title and a message.

▶ The title says 'Microsoft Excel'.

▶ The message says 'This value doesn't match the data validation restrictions defined for this cell.'

The title and the message are not very useful, are they? The title doesn't explain why the box appeared. The error message doesn't tell you why the data is wrong. This error message doesn't help you to enter valid data.

Choose a new error message

You can change the error message so it is more useful. Think about what data you want the user to enter:

▶ a number – no letters are allowed

▶ a whole number – with no decimal places

▶ positive numbers – no negative numbers are allowed.

The user needs to know this. Then they can enter the correct data.

Now you will plan a good error message for your validation rule. What important information does your user need to know? How can you give this information in clear words? Work in a group or with the whole class. Write down some ideas about what words to use.

The students at City Park School had a class discussion. They wrote down these ideas.

Don't type letters!	*Stock can't be a negative number.*
NUMBERS ONLY.	You should type a whole number only.
Integer data.	

Choose the error message that you like best. Or make up a message of your own. Remember the message needs a title and some message text.

Enter the error message

Now you will make the computer show the error message that you have chosen. You will use the same 'Data Validation' window that you used before.

▶ Select the cells where you have applied the validation rule (the 'Opening Stock', 'Stock in', and 'Stock out' fields).

▶ Click on the 'Data Validation' icon.

The 'Data Validation' window will open.

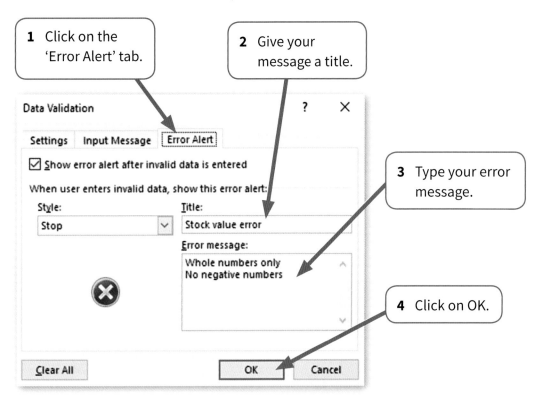

1 Click on the 'Error Alert' tab.

2 Give your message a title.

3 Type your error message.

4 Click on OK.

Test the error message

Now test your error message to make sure it works correctly. Try entering invalid data into your data table. You should see your error message.

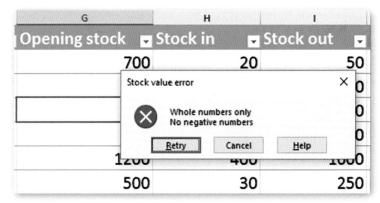

Add an input message

You can add a message for users to see before they enter data. This type of message is called an input message or an input prompt. The input message tells the user useful information about what they can input. It helps them to enter the correct input. It stops them from making mistakes. The input message should say:

▶ what data the user must input

▶ what data the user is not allowed to input.

Write down an input message for the stock fields.

Make the computer show your input message

Now you will make the computer show the input message you have chosen. To do this, you will use the 'Data Validation' window that you used before.

- ▶ Select the cells where you want your input message to appear (the same cells as before: 'Opening stock', 'Stock in' and 'Stock out').
- ▶ Click on the 'Data Validation' icon.
- ▶ Use the 'Data Validation' window to set the input message.

 **Activity**

Think of an error message for bad input and add this to the data table.

Think of an input message to help the user and add this to your data table.

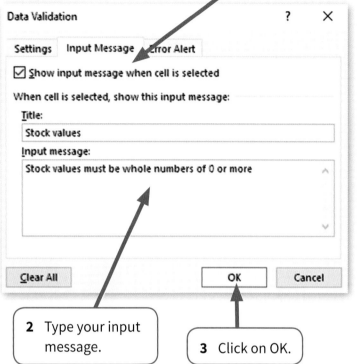

1 Click on the 'Input Message' tab.

2 Type your input message.

3 Click on OK.

 **Extra challenge**

In the last lesson you added a validation check to the 'Cost' field.
Now add an error message and an input message to this field, to help the user enter correct data.

 Test

1 When does the user see an error message?

2 How does a good error message help the user?

3 Think about the validation checks you have added to your data table in this lesson and the last lesson. Describe one data entry mistake which your validation checks would block.

4 An input message does not stop the user from entering bad data. How does it help to prevent errors?

 **Explore more**

Carry out research to find out what a QR code is. How can a business use a QR code in its warehouse for data entry? How will that improve data accuracy?

6 Numbers and data: Business data table

Check what you know

You have learned

▶ how to store data in a data table so people can access and use the data

▶ how to generate useful business information from a computer data table

▶ how to use error checks and error messages to block bad data.

Try the test and activities. They will help you to see how much you understand.

Test

A group of friends have started a savings club to help them save money. Each month they put some money into the club.

The friends use a data table to store information about the club members and how much money each member has saved. Here is an extract from their data table. The software has found and circled an error.

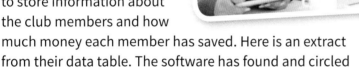

	A	B	C
1	**Saver ID** ▼	**Saver name** ▼	**Amount saved** ▼
2	S0001	Fareeza Bari	$ 340.00
3	S0002	Rashida Firman	$ 1,600.00
4	S0003	Lisa Huq	ABC
5	S0004	Mawara Khan	$ 3,000.00
6	S0005	Leona Martin	$ 540.00
7	S0006	Kelly Peters	$ 1,200.00

1 What is the name of the field that has an error?

2 What is the error in the data? Give an example of data that is allowed in this field.

3 How many fields are there in this data table?

4 The field 'Saver name' is not atomic. How can you improve this data table so that all the data is atomic?

5 Which of the fields in the data table is the key field?

6 What is the purpose of a key field in a data table?

⚙ Activities

1　Make a data table to store the savings club data. Use the data that you can see in the image on page 170.

　▶ Remember to use atomic fields.

　▶ Enter a valid savings amount for Lisa Huq.

2　Include a formula and a validation check.

　a　Format the 'Amount saved' data as currency.

　b　Enter a formula to add up the total amount saved by the members in the savings club.

　c　The only inputs allowed in the 'Amount saved' column are numbers. The numbers should be greater than or equal to 0. Add a validation check to this column to stop the user entering invalid data.

3　Include an input message.

　a　Add an input message to the amount saved column. The message should give helpful advice about the type of data input.

　b　Explain how you have reduced the chance of bad input to the spreadsheet.

Self-evaluation

● I answered test questions 1 and 2.

● I completed activity 1. I made a spreadsheet data table.

● I answered test questions 1–4.

● I completed activities 1 and 2. My spreadsheet data table included a formula and a validation check.

● I answered all the test questions.

● I completed all the activities. My spreadsheet table included an input message.

Re-read any parts of the unit you feel unsure about. Try the test and activities again – can you do more this time?

Glossary

ASCII a code used in computing that allows text and other characters to be represented in a computer as a binary code. ASCII only supports English language characters. ASCII stands for American Standard Code for Information Interchange

adware malware that causes unwanted adverts to be displayed on a computer

algorithm a plan to solve a problem. Programmers use algorithms when they plan programs

aligned arranged at one side of the available space. Text can be aligned on a page, or in a column or cell of a table

anti-virus (AV) software software designed to detect, block and quarantine malware

app short for application software; especially used to mean a small program you can run on your smartphone

application software a computer program that allows you to use your computer for a useful task

arithmetic operator an operator that transforms a value using the rules of maths – for example, addition or subtraction

assign set the value of a variable

atomic cannot be split up into smaller parts. Fields in a data table should be atomic – each field should store just a single item of data

attribution a citation that is in a form specified by the copyright holder

AutoSum a spreadsheet feature that adds together all the numbers in a column

binary a number system that uses only two digits, zero (0) and one (1)

bit each digit in a binary number

byte a group of eight bits used to store data in a computer

channel a source of sound that you record or hear. Headphones have two channels of audio: left and right. A radio or Wi-Fi speaker may have only one channel. Home cinema audio, often known as '5.1' or '7.1' surround sound systems, have up to eight channels and loudspeakers

citation a short piece of text that gives credit to the owner of any content that you have used in a document or on a web page

clip a single piece of audio or video content. Clips are often put together on a track or separate tracks to make a podcast or film

code a method of changing the characters in a message for other characters or symbols. Codes are used to disguise the meaning of messages or to convert information from one format to another

colour depth a measure of the quality of a digital image. Colour depth is the number of colours that can be used in a digital image. The more colours that can be used, the higher the colour depth and therefore the higher the quality of the image

comments lines of text in a program that the computer ignores. Programmers add comments to make their programs more readable for other programmers

compile turn source code into an executable file

compression a way of reducing the size of stored digital content (such as audio files) by removing some data from them. Compressed files can have be lower in quality. Lossless compression can avoid a loss in quality

conditional structure a programming structure that starts with the word 'if' and a logical test. The commands inside the structure are carried out if the test is True

cookie a file that a website creates on your computer when you visit the site. It may store information about you and your visit. The file is intended to make the website easier to use next time you visit the site

copyright the right to copy a piece of work. Copyright is usually held by the person who created the work

Creative Commons a method of licensing internet content such as images so that people can use them without asking the copyright holder

currency a data value that represents an amount of money. Currency values are often formatted with a currency symbol, such as $

cyberbully a person who uses the internet to frighten or intimidate another person

cybercrime crime committed with the help of the internet

cybercriminal a person who uses the internet to commit crime

data facts and figures. Data needs to be organised to make it useful

data format the style used to display data

data processing turning data into information that is useful. Computers are often used for data processing

data table a way of organising data to make it more useful. The data is stored in a grid of columns and rows. The columns are fields. The rows are records

digital made up of digits (number values)

digital data data that is converted into number values. Digital data can be stored and processed by a computer.

e-commerce any form of commerce (such as shopping or banking) that takes place over the internet

encrypt to code data so that if someone intercepts the data, they cannot read it or use it

error message a message that appears on the screen if you make a mistake in your program. It helps you find and fix the error

executable file a file of machine code commands that the computer can carry out

field a column in a data table. Each field stores one type of information

firewall software or hardware that blocks unauthorised access to a computer over the internet

float a number value with a decimal point

for loop the name for a counter-controlled loop in Python

frame a single still image that, together with many others, makes up an animation or video film

hacking breaking into a computer system without permission, usually to commit a crime or to damage data files

IDE (Integrated Development Environment) the software that you use to enter and save program commands. The IDE also runs the program

identity theft theft of personal details such as address or bank account details. The stolen information is used to commit fraud or theft

indent set in from the left margin. In Python, lines of code are indented to indicate structures such as loops

information data that has been organised to make it more useful

integer a whole number value without a decimal point

intellectual property something that a person has made using their mind and their creative talents

interface the part of a program that allows the user to interact with the program. The interface allows the user to enter inputs and it provides outputs

interpret turn source code into commands that the computer can run right away

JavaScript a programming language that works in a web browser

key field one of the fields in a data table. The key field stores data that is used to identify each record. The data in the key field is unique for each record. A product code number is an example of a key field

left-aligned aligned to the left of the page or cell. Any empty space appears on the right

logical error a type of programming error. The logic of the programming is wrong. The program doesn't do what the programmer intended

logical test a test that has the result True or False. Logical tests in programming usually compare two values using a relational operator

looped playback playing back part of an audio clip over and over again. This is helpful when you are trying to find mistakes

machine code a command language the computer understands. Machine code is made of code numbers. Each code number stands for a different action

malware software installed on a computer without the user's knowledge, designed to damage the user's computer or to steal data

mix control the loudness and effects on each track in a digital audio workstation so that the tracks form a pleasing sound

mono a recording that uses a single channel of audio. The sound is not separated into a Left and Right channel as for stereo recordings

multi-track a recording with clips on more than one track. The clips can play at the same time; for example, one clip could be background music

operator a symbol or term in programming that transforms values

overflow an error that is caused when a computer attempts to store a value in an area of memory that is too small

parameters settings that control a feature or a process in a software app, for example, to control an effect in a digital audio workstation

phishing using fake emails and websites to trick people into giving up their passwords and other personal data

pixel a picture element, the smallest element of a digital image. A pixel is a single colour

plagiarism using another person's work but claiming it as your own

podcast a sound recording similar to a radio programme that is shared over the web. Podcasts are usually made as a series of episodes. They can be published daily, weekly or monthly

programming language a system of words and operators used to write computer programs

Python Shell the window you see when you start Python. You can enter commands in the Python Shell one at a time and see the result of each command

quarantine a method used by anti-virus software to make malware harmless. When the AV software detects a malware signature in a file, the AV software quarantines the file so it cannot be opened

ransomware a type of malware that blocks a user's access to the files on their computer. A ransom is usually demanded to restore access to files

readable easy for other programmers to read and understand – used to describe program code

record a row in a data table. Each record stores all the information about one item

registration entering personal details to become a member of a website. A registered user is able to log in to the site and access services that only members can use

requirement a statement that tells you what a program should do. You write the program based on the requirement

resolution a measure of the quality of a digital image. Resolution is the number of pixels used in a digital image. The higher the number of pixels, the higher the resolution and therefore the higher the quality of the image

right-aligned aligned to the right of the page or cell. Any empty space appears on the left

run carry out the commands in a program

safety copy a copy of a file you make before you start editing the content. If you make a mistake, you can return to the safety copy and start again

sampling a method of capturing continuous data (such as sound) and converting it to digital data

scamming using fake emails or websites to steal money from internet users

secure site a website that uses encryption so that that messages sent over the internet are secure

signature a small fragment of code contained in a piece of malware, used by anti-virus software to detect the malware

software a program you can run on your computer. The program has been turned into machine code so your computer can understand it

source code a program written in a programming language

spyware malware that records a user's activity on a computer and sends a record of the user's actions over the internet to a cybercriminal. Spyware can be used to capture passwords and other personal information

stream listen to or watch media content such as audio or video by receiving it in a continuous stream from the internet, instead of downloading a copy of the file to your own device

string a data value that is made of text characters. The characters can be any keyboard characters, including letters and digits

syntax the rules of a language, for example, the rules of a programming language

syntax error a type of programming error. The program breaks the rules of the programming language

track a section of an audio project that holds audio clips that play one after the other. A multi-track recording has more than one track that you can edit separately

translate turn source code into machine code

trim shorten clips of audio or video using editing software

trojan a piece of malware that is hidden inside a data file or software app

true colour a method used by computers to create and store lifelike images

Unicode a code similar to ASCII code. Unicode can represent many more characters than ASCII. Unicode supports many languages, including Arabic and Mandarin

user friendly easy and enjoyable to use – often used to describe the features of a program

validation a way of checking data accuracy. Validation uses rules to check the data. If the data breaks the rules it cannot be entered into a data table

value a number that can be used in arithmetic and logical calculations

virus a piece of malware that infects any file it comes into contact with, causing the malware to spread

while loop the name for a condition-controlled loop in Python